# IT'S MY WHOLE LIFE

# SUSAN WIDER

# IT'S MY WHOLE LIFE

## CHARLOTTE SALOMON: AN ARTIST IN HIDING DURING WORLD WAR II

**NORTON YOUNG READERS**
An Imprint of W. W. Norton & Company
Independent Publishers Since 1923

To Bill, who always sees the possibilities.

To Sarah, who understands in ways only a sister can.

And to my father, Captain Henry Wider (1921–2003),
United States Army, Bronze Star,
who wanted to help all the Charlottes.

Copyright © 2022 by Susan Wider

All rights reserved
Printed in the United States of America
First Edition

For information about permission to reproduce selections from this book, write to
Permissions, W. W. Norton & Company, Inc., 500 Fifth Avenue, New York, NY 10110

For information about special discounts for bulk purchases, please contact
W. W. Norton Special Sales at specialsales@wwnorton.com or 800-233-4830

Manufacturing by Versa Press
Book design by Hana Anouk Nakamura
Production manager: Beth Steidle

ISBN 978-1-324-01545-1

W. W. Norton & Company, Inc., 500 Fifth Avenue, New York, N.Y. 10110
www.wwnorton.com

W. W. Norton & Company Ltd., 15 Carlisle Street, London W1D 3BS

0  9  8  7  6  5  4  3  2  1

# CONTENTS

Charlotte Salomon, self-portrait from *Life?* or *Theater?*

# PROLOGUE

The doctor's house in the South of France had a small cellar with no light. In a dusty corner in autumn 1943, an enormous suitcase waited in the gloom, its remarkable contents hidden from the world. Only three people knew about the contents:

    **—the first was a twenty-six-year-old artist and writer;**

    **—the second was her husband;**

    **—the third was the doctor himself.**

The three were friends. They were trying to help one another survive in what had been a lively, festive resort on the southern French coast. Now the town of Villefranche-sur-Mer found itself overtaken by World War II. It had been safe there when each of the three individuals had arrived, separately and unacquainted. Refugees from throughout Europe fled to France to escape Adolf Hitler's soldiers, but his war of evil and extermination would not go away.

In mid-1943, the young artist had carried the suitcase's precious contents through increasingly dangerous streets. When she arrived at the home of her family doctor and friend, she gave him several wrapped parcels and asked him to protect her secrets.

This is the story of those secrets.

CHAPTER ONE

# DENIED

*The artistic abilities of the full Jew Fräulein*
*Salomon are beyond doubt.*
—Admissions Committee, Vereinigte Staatsschulen
für freie und angewandte Kunst, Berlin

Twenty-year-old Charlotte Salomon walked toward Steinplatz square. She was headed for the large, gray, four-story building up ahead, Berlin's Vereinigte Staatsschulen für freie und angewandte Kunst (known today as Unitersität der Künste Berlin, University of the Arts Berlin). She entered the building between its two front entrance columns, passing beneath the three Latin words carved over the door frame: ERUDIENDAE ARTIBUS IUVENTUTI (Instructing Youth in the Arts). Above the encouraging words hung a Nazi flag, fluttering black, white, and blood red in the soft breeze. Charlotte was Jewish in Adolf Hitler's Berlin in 1937 and one of only a small number of Jews in the entire school.

Charlotte was on her way to Professor Ludwig Bartning's

Vereinigte Staatsschulen, Steinplatz building, Berlin 1930.

drawing class. She wore her usual color choice, gray, the same color as most of her paintings. Once inside her classroom, she mumbled a tiny hello and took her seat. But today's class was different. With his too-large, white painting smock flapping loosely as he gestured, Professor Bartning asked his students to draw a still-life picture using vases, bowls, whatever they wanted from the *Requisitenkammer*, the prop room. He said the pictures would be exhibited later, and that the students were not to sign them.

For an earlier assignment Professor Bartning had asked them to illustrate fairy tales. Charlotte and her friend Barbara—one of her few friends there—had painted together. Charlotte's pictures flowed with abstract shapes. Barbara drew events from her own childhood, painting watercolor sequences across the page with

Charlotte walks toward the art school entrance.

narration on the back. Perhaps Charlotte made a mental note of that in order to experiment with Barbara's approach later.

Charlotte finished her still-life painting and left the art room with her classmates. Then the classroom door was closed.

The "assignment" was actually a blind competition for a prize, but the students didn't know that. After deliberation, the professors announced Barbara's picture as the winner. Barbara was a tall blonde and blue-eyed beauty, an ideal German, or "Aryan," girl. *Aryan* was the term Adolf Hitler had borrowed from the Sanskrit language to describe the pure German race he intended to create. But first, he had to purge Germany of people he felt were undesirable, like Jews, Gypsies, homosexuals, Catholics, physically disabled people, and more. Barbara had the perfect German appearance that Hitler prized for his Master Race.

But Barbara's victory in the contest was a lie. Charlotte's still-life drawing had been voted the winner, until the teachers realized that the picture was created by a Jew. Barbara thought the teachers did this to protect Charlotte, to keep her Jewish name out of the newspapers as the prize winner.

Not long after the teachers announced to everyone that Barbara had won the contest, they also told Charlotte that she could no longer associate with the other students. If she wanted to continue at the school, she would be allowed only to paint there at night. Charlotte walked through the building toward the school's entrance, toward light and air. This was not the first time she had been denied something because she was Jewish. In Herr Hitler's Germany, Jews were bullied all the time. They could no

Charlotte's friend Barbara Petzel.

longer sit on park benches, go to swimming pools, or use public transportation. But to be severed like this from her art studies must have been a blow to her heart.

---

Qualifying for admission to the Vereinigte Staatsschulen (VS) had not been easy for Charlotte. In autumn 1933, at age sixteen, before she could even begin to think about applying to the VS, she first had to grapple with fashion school, her stepmother Paula's idea. When Charlotte had originally explained to Paula how badly she wanted to go to art school, Paula enrolled her in Berlin's Feige-Strassburger fashion drawing school for Jewish girls—not at all what Charlotte was hoping for. A career in art made sense to Paula only if the artist earned money. Paula had great respect for wealthy people. She made this clear to Charlotte. The fashion school director, in turn, was happy to accept Charlotte, assuring Paula that Charlotte would be earning a good living soon.

Charlotte sat in her classroom, with its yellow walls and grimy windows, learning about fashion drawing. She was miserable. The other students laughed at her for wearing plain clothes—it was fashion school, after all—and not dressing up for school parties. At home in the evenings, she sat with her head in her hands, fighting headaches and thinking about why the people at the school were so "widerlich" (disgusting). Paula's plan was not working.

Charlotte's maternal grandparents offered her a rescue scheme by inviting her to visit them in Rome for her seventeenth birthday, in April 1934. Grandmother and Grandfather Grunwald had moved to Italy the previous autumn because Grandmother was afraid to live in Berlin with the Nazis coming to power. Adolf Hitler had been appointed *Reichskanzler*, chancellor of Germany, in January 1933. By the end of the year, he had reconfigured his country into a dictatorship. The Grunwalds first did some traveling in Italy and then settled in Rome. They seemed overly eager to cheer Charlotte up after fashion school and she wondered at the nervousness of their concern. She had no way of knowing that they feared for her health and safety because of terrible family secrets. But Italy had to be better than dreary Berlin.

Charlotte had visited Italy as a child, but this was her first trip as a young adult. She made discovery after discovery. With her grandparents she visited the Colosseum, with its rows of weathered stone archways reaching into the blue sky. They viewed the Roman Forum, where Charlotte studied the ruins of ancient Ionic (scroll-topped) columns, storing up ideas of shapes and textures for her own paintings. The white dome of St. Peter's Basilica, the triangular roof detail of the Pantheon, and the rich golds and yellows of Italian stonework all found their way into her art.

Charlotte also had opportunities to see famous Italian paintings. "Michelangelo is fabulous," she wrote later, "so much power. I have to contort my neck to see it properly, but it's worth it." Rome made a lasting impression on Charlotte, and she regretted leaving the clear skies and the transparent quality of light to return to the gray of Berlin.

Back at fashion school, things did not get better. Charlotte's teacher had nothing nice to say about her work, even going so far as to tell her she had no talent at all. She left fashion school and decided to apply for serious art studies at the VS, which she called the Academy. The entrance exam was coming up. "Only he who dares can win," she wrote. "Only he who dares can begin." *Nur der wagt,* "only he who dares."

The entrance exam was awful. Charlotte sat with her drawing board and paper on her lap. She was surrounded by the other hopeful candidates—including several young men in Nazi uniforms—all drawing intently and diligently. She couldn't see straight. The male model they were meant to draw looked slumped, dark, and sickly to her. She didn't manage to put anything successful on her paper. "Oh I'm trying, but in vain!" she wrote in rhyme. "My lovely dream is down the drain! Not for me—Academy." She was right. The professor overseeing the exam told her that her work was unsatisfactory. Dejected, she asked him if she should continue to paint at home. He said it was her choice.

Charlotte was not giving up. After her failure at the exam, she knew she had to talk to her father. She explained to him, in a flood of tears, how badly she still wanted art lessons. First, he comforted her. Then he agreed. When her stepmother, Paula, protested that he was wasting money on Charlotte's lack of talent, he silenced her. "If she's that keen on it," Charlotte remembered him saying, "she should have lessons." He thought that a good education was the best way to help his daughter.

Charlotte began her studies with a private teacher, not long after failing the VS exam. Unlike the instructors at fashion school, this teacher was stylish and meticulous. She wore her reddish-golden hair braided into a fashionable low chignon at the back

Charlotte pleads for art lessons; Paula says she has no talent.

Charlotte practices painting.

of her neck, and she dressed in vivid reds and blues. Charlotte found her to be very demanding. One day, slumped at her desk in the teacher's light-filled studio, Charlotte stared at a potted plant sitting in front of her. She had already drawn the little plant ten times, but the teacher had erased every try and made her start over. Charlotte couldn't figure out what she was doing wrong. Was it the shape of the leaves? The curve of the pot? The wrong type of pencil stroke? Finally, the teacher stopped tormenting Charlotte and explained that she had miscounted the number of leaves on the plant. Her next try, which incorporated every last leaf, was met with "I really think you have a nice little gift."

Charlotte had the ability to focus intensely and could draw for hours on end, losing track of time and her surroundings. She created drawings and paintings of leggy, twisted plants; large golden sunflowers; clusters of white daisies; and red and yellow tulips. She worked on still-life pictures with vases of flowers and bowls of fruit. She drew household items like toys and dolls, even work boots. She experimented with using deep teals and burgundies, and making curved, fluid shapes. Pictures flew off her easel.

By the autumn of 1935, when Charlotte was eighteen, she was ready to end her private studies and tackle the VS entrance exam again. She was surrounded once more by candidates, but this time things were clear in Charlotte's head. Her training and hard work had prepared her for a more successful attempt. She studied the male model standing on the raised platform and her right hand flowed easily across the paper on her drawing board. This model looked strong, muscular, and healthy, and so did her drawing. She paid no attention to what the girl next to her was doing; she just focused on her subject and let her hand fly free. "Ja, diesmal geht's," she wrote (Yes, this time it's going well).

The VS had a quota for Jewish students that was limited to only 1.5 percent of the total student body. But Charlotte had the support of VS painting and drawing teacher Professor Ludwig Bartning. She also gained support from the admissions committee because she was "modest and reserved." They felt she would not "present a danger to the Aryan male students." In other words, she wouldn't seem tempting or desirable to the young men in her classes. The Master Race was not in danger of being diluted. Charlotte was admitted.

## CHAPTER TWO

# GOVERNED

*No one can possibly cope with such a brat.*

—one of Charlotte's governesses

Charlotte had loved to draw from the time she was around nine or ten years old. It all started with the only governess she ever liked—and the only one she picked for herself.

She and Grandmother and Grandfather Grunwald were on one of their regular holidays in Italy, renting a small, isolated house in the country. Charlotte spotted a young woman sitting in a meadow full of flowers, playing a lute. There was a small child next to the woman and the craggy, knife-edged Dolomite Mountains of northern Italy loomed over the meadow. Even as a child Charlotte loved Italy. And she perhaps saw something to love in this woman. Charlotte persuaded her grandparents to hire her as a governess. A month later, the woman, and her lute, came to live with the family in Berlin. Charlotte called her Hase, which means "hare" in German, but her full name and life story are lost.

Hase had a kind face and gentle manner and Charlotte learned from her. Hase told Charlotte she had a gift for drawing. She taught her how to hold and use a paintbrush, and how to mix and blend colors, and Charlotte was hooked. Her first painting was of a little boy running after a big yellow church bell. Hase and Charlotte sat together and sketched during trips to the seaside. One of Charlotte's first portraits—of many hundreds over her lifetime—was of Hase wearing a cherry-red dress.

Before Hase, there had been a parade of governesses through the Salomon apartment in Berlin. "I don't need any governesses," Charlotte remembered saying. "I know by myself what I want." But in they came, and Charlotte had great fun tormenting them. She boasted about inventing "all kinds of naughtiness." One slapped her and told Grandmother that coping with such an unruly child was impossible. When that one left, Charlotte was delighted. But she wrote that the next one was worse and insisted that Charlotte "do as I say—right now!" Charlotte did not.

It hadn't always been like this. Before the chain of governesses, there had been Charlotte's own mother. The beautiful Franziska.

Franziska Grunwald was born on July 25, 1890, in Berlin, the eldest daughter of Marianne and Ludwig Grunwald. She had a younger sister by five years who died at only age eighteen. Franziska had adored her sister, whose name was also Charlotte.

Near the beginning of World War I, Franziska became a nurse and fell in love with a young surgeon she enjoyed assisting in the operating room, even dabbing at his runny nose during surgery. His name was Albert Salomon. The day he came to the Grunwalds' apartment, bringing lilacs and a marriage proposal,

Aunt Charlotte; Charlotte's mother, Franziska; and their parents,
Ludwig and Marianne Grunwald.

The Salomons' apartment building, Wielandstrasse 15, Berlin.

was a stressful one for Franziska. She had told her parents all about this talented doctor and had explained how much she loved him, but the Grunwalds worried he wasn't good enough for their daughter. He was terribly shy, and he didn't appear to be very wealthy. But Franziska got her way and the couple married on her birthday in 1916.

Even though the wedding took place during the war, Franziska's white gown was splendid, and her bouquet of roses was enormous. The candlelit banquet was lavish, with tubs of rose trees decorating the room, and an army of servants scurrying about, looking after the guests. The Grunwalds remained somber, in keeping with the wartime mood outside their doors. They were also still concerned about Albert's finances, and were worried about Franziska's health because she sometimes suffered from depression.

Interior of the Salomon home, as painted by Charlotte.

Franziska and Albert spent their wedding night in an expensive Berlin hotel, but Albert had to leave the next morning to return to his war work as a surgeon in a military hospital in France. The Grunwalds wanted Franziska to come home with them, but she preferred to move directly into her new home. Her disobedience angered the Grunwalds.

The apartment was large, with a medical consulting room and a study for Albert. There was a formal blue living room with Franziska's grand piano. The large dining room also contained a small alcove for breakfast and afternoon tea. A long hallway led to the linen room, with closets full of sheets, towels, and tablecloths for every occasion. The remaining rooms included a big kitchen, a master bedroom, a bathroom, and the maid's quarters. And, of course, a nursery.

By the time Franziska and Albert were close to celebrating their first wedding anniversary, they were also celebrating the birth of their daughter on April 16, 1917. They named the baby Charlotte in memory of Franziska's younger sister, who had died in 1913. Franziska was delighted with little Charlotte, even though the baby cried endlessly. The family hired a nurse to care for Charlotte, but Franziska preferred to do much of the work herself. Charlotte grew up in a home where her parents loved her, played with her, took her on wonderful vacations, and surrounded her with celebrations for every special occasion. Theirs was an assimilated Jewish family. This meant that they lived like their non-Jewish friends and neighbors did, eating the same foods and celebrating the same holidays, even Christmas.

When Charlotte was around six, Franziska took her to begin

Charlotte paints scenes of her life as a baby.

Scenes from grade school and childhood.

Charlotte at around age eight, 1925.

grade school in Bleibtreustrasse, two blocks away. The pupils sat on hard benches at a long table, with Charlotte near one end and the teacher at the other. This was unfortunate because Charlotte liked to observe and take in all the details of her environment. But with the teacher at the other end of the table, Charlotte was always in her line of sight. Every time Charlotte glanced around the room or at her fellow pupils, she received stern reprimands.

Near Charlotte sat curly, dark-haired Kurt, her best friend. When they weren't at school, Charlotte and Kurt played games together outdoors or went tobogganing or, Charlotte's favorite, ice-skating. At home, she had plenty of toys. There were dolls, a scooter, even a toy car big enough to ride in.

When Charlotte was around eight years old, something shifted. Franziska began telling her daughter stories about Heaven, explaining that things were much more beautiful there. She talked about going to Heaven and then writing Charlotte a letter to describe it all. Charlotte would snuggle into her mother's bed with her and hear about life after death and how wonderful it would be to have her mother become an angel. Charlotte loved her mother, and accepted what she said.

Soon after these bedtime conversations started, Charlotte

Charlotte and her Grunwald grandparents
stay home during her mother's funeral.

began to notice that her mother seemed unhappy. Franziska still played the piano, took singing lessons, helped her husband with his medical practice, and gave splendid dinner parties. But Charlotte saw a change. Why did her mother talk about death all the time? Why did she seem so sad? Why did she say she was so alone when she had a daughter and a husband who loved her? Without explanation, her mother was suddenly whisked away to stay with Grandmother and Grandfather Grunwald at their apartment on Kochstrasse, about four miles away. Charlotte and her father went for occasional visits, and Charlotte always saw a nurse in the room with her mother.

A telephone call near the end of February in 1926 brought terrible news from the Grunwalds. Charlotte heard the phone ring, then heard her father say something about losing "her" and that his happiness was gone. Charlotte was told that Franziska had died from the flu.

Charlotte sat between Grandmother and Grandfather on the dark brown couch in her grandparents' apartment, no bright colors here, just ugly-green carpet and somber reddish-brown wood paneling on the walls. Charlotte wanted to know why everyone was crying. She reasoned that her mother was probably very happy since she had told Charlotte she wanted to be an angel in Heaven, and that must be where she had gone.

Her grandparents described losing their daughter. And then it dawned on Charlotte that she had lost her mother. A few weeks later, Charlotte visited Franziska's grave with her father and grandparents. She placed a letter to her mother near the gravestone. In the envelope was a reminder to write soon and tell her all about Heaven. Every night Charlotte went to her bedroom window at least ten times to look for her mother's reply on the windowsill. Nothing. She could not sleep she was so disappointed.

Franziska had broken her promise.

## CHAPTER THREE

# ABANDONED

*And I was left with this child.*

—Grandmother Grunwald speaking about Charlotte

Nine-year-old Charlotte locked herself in her grandparents' bathroom, sat on the edge of the tub, and stared at the toilet. Mother was gone. Father was sad and much too busy. Grandmother and Grandfather were as terse and dreary as ever. And Charlotte had just felt that thing again—"something terrible, with skeleton's limbs," she called it. She had started seeing this frightening red-and-dark-blue shape in a hallway at her grandparents' apartment, not long after leaving the letter at her mother's grave. She felt panicked in the dark and gloomy corridor, and always ran as fast as she could to get out of there. She feared that the vision had something to do with her mother.

In April 1927, Charlotte turned ten. It was just over a year since her mother's death, and she had survived the string of

Charlotte with her father, around 1927.

unpleasant governesses and was now settled in with her father and Hase at the Berlin apartment. Hase's role as governess meant being a companion to Charlotte, but also included acting as a replacement mother by helping Charlotte with her bath and putting her to bed.

The Salomon apartment was at Wielandstrasse 15 in Berlin's Charlottenburg district, a neighborhood full of successful businesspeople, intellectuals, and artists. Charlotte had finished grade school and now attended the Fürstin-Bismarck-Gymnasium (today called the Sophie-Charlotte-Gymnasium), a secondary school for well-to-do girls in Sybelstrasse around the corner from the family's apartment.

Most children began their *Gymnasium* studies at age ten and continued for about nine years. Charlotte's best subjects were religion, German, drawing, and sports. She wore a school uniform: a long-sleeved white blouse with a button-down collar, a dark necktie, and a short pleated skirt. Charlotte was easily a head taller than other girls in her class, which meant that her standard-uniform pleats stopped well above her bony knees.

She had a new friend at school named Hilde. After class they sometimes went to the home of Grandmother's best friend, whom Charlotte called Aunt Martha (her real name is unknown). "Aunt Martha" had a beautiful garden, a greenhouse, orchards, and cows that the girls would milk. There was also a tennis court where Charlotte and Hilde played singles together. They changed out of their school uniforms into white tennis dresses that looked like sailor suits, with matching orange neckerchiefs and belts. Charlotte became a very good tennis player. She stopped checking her bedroom windowsill for letters from her mother in Heaven, and she was happier at school.

In 1928, Hase and Charlotte went to Sylt Island in the North Sea, Germany's northernmost island, where they played on the twenty-five-mile-long beach, swam in the sea, and continued to draw and paint. Hase let Charlotte go horseback riding by herself on the beach, and even let her ride bareback.

For several years after his wife's death, Charlotte's father seemed distant to her. He immersed himself in his medical research and teaching at the university. Like Charlotte, he had lost his mother too. She had died after giving birth to Albert. Because his father was a merchant in Röbel, Germany, about halfway between Berlin and Hamburg, Albert was raised by relatives. He was only seventeen when he moved to Berlin to study medicine. Nine years later, in 1909, he began work as a surgeon at the university hospital in Berlin.

Albert developed innovative surgical methods for cancer treatment and was the first physician to identify breast cancer from X-rays. (Today, Albert Salomon is considered a pioneer of mammography.) Charlotte was very proud of her father, but all his hard work meant spending a lot of time away from her.

But during family vacations, Charlotte could be with him more. In 1929, soon after she turned twelve, they visited Italy and then Switzerland. Charlotte, her father, her grandparents, and Hase traveled by train to Venice, where Charlotte felt very much at home. Her grandparents took time to tell her about the places they would visit so that she was knowledgeable and prepared for what she was about to see. She appreciated standing among the army of pigeons in Saint Mark's Square to admire the pointed, red-brick bell tower because she had already been told about it. She studied the Gothic arches of the nearby, dazzling-white Doge's Palace on the Grand Canal, and would later re-create them in her paintings.

On their last morning in Venice, Charlotte sneaked out of the hotel because she wanted to memorize some of the city landmarks before she had to leave them behind. She tried to draw Saint Mark's Basilica and then

Charlotte (standing, right) and classmates at the Fürstin-Bismarck school, around 1933, including Hilde (standing, left) and Marianne (standing, center).

saw her father, who was also out early, capturing the sights with his camera. When father and daughter returned hand in hand to their hotel they were met by a distraught Grandmother, who was furious with both of them for each going out on their own.

After the trip, when Charlotte returned to Berlin and to school, she found that Hilde had a new best friend named Marianne, and the two girls were not interested in a three-way friendship.

Hase and Charlotte, Sylt Island, 1928.

For a while Charlotte followed them around, trying to fit in, but when that didn't work, she kept to herself. She read romance novels, played Ping-Pong, and welcomed gym class as a distraction, especially the parallel bars. She let her hair grow long and spent hours styling it, standing in front of the full-length mirror in her room. And she always found plenty of time for her drawing.

Albert had a new distraction too; he decided to start dating. "He is a lover of fine food," Charlotte wrote, "and also thinks it would be a good idea to remarry, only that the choice . . . is quite difficult."

The beautiful opera singer with the long blonde curls came to their apartment nearly every evening. Albert had met her at a party where he heard her sing music by Franz Schubert. Was he falling in love with her voice, or with everything about her? Twelve-year-old Charlotte couldn't answer for her father, but she looked forward to the famous Paula Lindberg's visits at least as much as he did, maybe more. Charlotte liked having this strong, intelligent woman in her life. She had a soft motherly face under all those curls, and she paid attention to Charlotte. After Charlotte's bath

Charlotte's portrayal of Sylt Island in the North Sea, with Hase.

Paula (Levi) Lindberg, around the time Charlotte met her.

in the evening, Hase would put Charlotte to bed and then Paula would come into Charlotte's room, sit on the edge of the bed, and hold her hand. Perhaps Paula sang to her or told her bedtime stories. Charlotte wanted to tell Paula how much she liked having her there, and how she looked forward to the visits, but she was too shy to say even a word about what she was feeling.

Paula Lindberg was born Paula Levi in 1897 near Mannheim, Germany. She was fourteen years younger than Albert Salomon and seven years younger than Charlotte's own mother would have been. Paula was the only child of Jewish rabbi Lazarus Levi and his wife, Sophie Meyer. Rabbi Levi wanted Paula to become a mathematics teacher, and she tried. She studied mathematics in the nearby town of Heidelberg right after World War I. But when her father died suddenly at the end of 1919 at only age fifty-seven, Paula quickly abandoned her mathematics courses and switched to studying voice at a music school in Mannheim. This also did not last long. She was such a talented singer that the famous German orchestra conductor and composer Wilhelm Furtwängler recommended she move to Berlin to study at the music academy there, where she changed

Opera singer Paula.

her last name to Lindberg to protect herself from anti-Semitism. Her performances and her personality soon became highlights of Berlin's music scene.

Paula did more than spend evenings at the Salomon apartment. She showed up at Albert and Charlotte's hotel during a father-daughter trip to the Rhine River valley. Paula even sang for them in the hotel's red-carpeted lobby. Later, at dinner, with Hase nowhere in sight, Albert and Paula let Charlotte have some wine, which she was not used to drinking. The wine loosened Charlotte's tongue and she told Paula about the other women her father had been dating, and described all the presents they brought for her. Albert was embarrassed, but Paula was enchanted.

Charlotte played the recording over and over on the family phonograph. She couldn't get enough of hearing Paula's deep, rich contralto voice singing an aria from Georges Bizet's opera *Carmen*. She played the record so much that it began to get stuck after every few bars of music, causing one or two syllables to repeat annoyingly. Charlotte had to stand next to the phonograph and constantly rescue the needle, every time it faltered, physically lifting it and moving it forward.

It was September 1930 and Paula and Albert had gone to Paula's hometown near Mannheim to be married, since Paula's mother still lived there. Thirteen-year-old Charlotte stayed behind in Berlin with her grandparents, Hase, and the precious recording of Paula.

The marriage was not the only new development in Charlotte's world.

"Our home is being all changed around," she wrote, "and I have to give up my room to her [Paula], and my dear Hase is leaving me." With Paula as her new stepmother, there was no longer any need for Hase. Other household staff were being replaced as well. "Those new ones are coming," wrote Charlotte, not sure who they were or what they would be like. Eventually Charlotte consoled herself with the thought that Paula would be her new mother, and everyone loved Paula, "but no one as much as I do" (*keiner so wie ich*), she wrote, quoting from an operetta by Franz Lehar.

When Paula and Albert returned to Berlin after a honeymoon in Italy, Charlotte's adoration of Paula continued. In school she was so lost in her thoughts of Paula that she couldn't pay attention in class. When she returned to the apartment after school each day, her first question was "Ist 'Sie' zu Haus?" (Is "she" at home?). Charlotte even felt jealous of her father.

For Paula's next birthday, in December 1930, Charlotte went to an elegant Berlin store to buy a powder compact as a birthday gift. She stayed up all night looking at it and couldn't wait to give it to Paula the next morning with a big bouquet of flowers. Paula hugged Charlotte tenderly, with thanks and love. Later that day Charlotte rushed home from school only to find that Paula had a visitor and no time for Charlotte. She was disappointed that she would have to wait.

Paula also loved having large dinner parties at home. Charlotte didn't like them because she wanted Paula for herself.

One evening, after about two dozen dinner guests had finally left, Charlotte's obvious delight at seeing them go annoyed Paula enough to cause their first fight, ending in tears for both.

Charlotte snuggled into the plush crimson seat next to her father in the big concert hall. She wore a sky-blue dress, and her haircut was short and simple. She watched the members of the symphony orchestra as they took their seats on the stage, their lustrous instruments gleaming. Although not yet fourteen, Charlotte had already taken piano lessons and singing lessons, and she had a musical ear.

She and her father were waiting for the concert to begin so that Charlotte could hear Paula perform with an orchestra. Finally, the lights dimmed, the audience quieted down, and the orchestra conductor and Paula walked onstage. Paula wore a burgundy gown that emphasized all her curves. Her blond curls were arranged softly around her face, and she had draped a lace shawl over her shoulders. The glorious tone of Paula's voice soaring over the rich music from the orchestra seemed like colors to Charlotte. She saw blues and reds and yellows showering over her. She used this idea later in her paintings. She made dozens of short brushstrokes in these happy colors that cascaded outward from the musicians' instruments and arced over the audience.

The parade of Nazi soldiers in the street below the apartment windows looked like a sea of orange to fifteen-year-old Charlotte.

Charlotte and her father attend one of Paula's performances.

It was late January 1933. The marching footfalls slapped in loud unison on the pavement. Above the soldiers' heads, their large, red Nazi flag whipped erratically, with its black spiderlike swastika symbol crawling across it. (Hitler borrowed the symbol from Eurasian cultures to represent national German pride.) Charlotte's sixteenth birthday was still three months away, but suddenly she was dealing with terrifying developments.

Many important jobs in businesses and in government were held by Jews, who were now being abused, called *Judenschwein*, "Jewish pigs." Germans who did business with them were called *Schwein* too. Nazi propaganda had convinced some of the German people that Jews had betrayed, cheated, and deceived them, and they began to boycott and vandalize Jewish businesses. Charlotte sensed that these Germans thought their lives would not improve unless Jews were killed. But she later wrote that Jews "were both human and Jewish!"

On March 29, 1933, Albert came home from his job at the University of Berlin Medical School with the news that he had been fired. Jews were being dismissed from jobs throughout the country. How could Albert continue his groundbreaking breast cancer research? How would he be able to teach medical students about his ideas to save patients' lives?

Not long after this, Paula was bullied at one of her performances. As her voice blended with the lush orchestral accompaniment there was angry shouting mixed with the music, coming from inside the concert hall. "Aus—Raus—Aus—Raus" (Out—get out—out—get out). This time the music would not have sounded like red, yellow, and blue color splashes to Charlotte. The

Nazi march in Berlin, 1933.

conductor, Paula, and the orchestra were taunted into abandoning the stage. The concert was over.

What would Jews like Albert and Paula do without their jobs and careers? Albert had only one choice: Berlin's Jewish hospital. As a Jew, he was allowed to work there, so at least he was still getting paid. Things were harder for Paula. Eventually she found work with the Jüdischer Kulturbund (Jewish Culture League), a sponsoring organization for Jewish artists to express their creativity and talents, and to earn money. They used small theaters, community centers, synagogues, and private homes for their performances. The audiences were exclusively Jewish, and subscribers paid a membership fee for the right to buy tickets for two events of their choice per month.

The growing violence and segregation had an impact on Charlotte, too. She was still at the Fürstin-Bismarck Gymnasium. In spite of the school's motto, "To Unite You Not in Hatred but in Love," Jewish students were bullied by the non-Jews and by some of the teachers. Daily fights took place in the streets, where Nazi youth waited for the Jewish students to arrive so they could tear their clothes or beat them up. Several of the girls, who had been raised as Christians in German Jewish households where Judaism was not practiced, didn't even know they were Jewish until the school required all students to present identification papers. Some of the other girls' mothers refused to let them have Jewish friends.

With her dark-blonde hair, slender build, rosy cheeks, and round German face, Charlotte didn't "look" Jewish. And she hadn't been raised Jewish; her family even celebrated Christmas. Above all, she just felt . . . *human*. She was also very close to graduating and receiving her *Abitur*, the university entrance qualification. Without that, she would lose any chance of going to college.

In the end, Charlotte didn't care about the *Abitur*. She told her father that she would not return to school in autumn of 1933 and that she wanted to learn to draw. Ever since Hase, she had loved drawing and painting, but she had never had formal art lessons.

"Just see your finals through," she remembered her father telling her.

Charlotte made her own decision, disobeyed her father, and quit school at age sixteen.

With more time spent at home, she began to see changes in her adored stepmother. It seemed to Charlotte that Paula had too many friends and too many charitable activities, and too much stress. Charlotte particularly disliked Paula's attempts to control her. In her memoir, Charlotte wrote at length about these changes:

> *Spurred on by her many admirers, she has acquired an exalted opinion of herself in common with everyone else. . . . She believes that, purified by much suffering, she is now one of the most admirable human specimens. . . . Her glorious voice no longer possessed the same warm, expressive tone. . . . If anyone had come and dared to raise the least doubt about her life or about her singing, she would no doubt have laughed in his face. So convinced was she of her own glory [so überzeugt war sie von eigener Herrlichkeit].*

Charlotte was losing her adoration for Paula.

## CHAPTER FOUR

# COACHED

*He's just as crazy as you are.*

—Paula, describing Alfred Wolfsohn to Charlotte

The man with the wild, curly dark hair and the huge, black round glasses was back. Charlotte had glimpsed him coming and going from Paula's music room for days, but she hadn't been introduced to him yet. Paula was also assisting the Künstlerhilfe der Jüdischen Gemeinde zu Berlin (Berlin Jewish Community's Artists Aid). The Künstlerhilfe director had sent the man to Paula and asked her to evaluate his knowledge as a singing coach.

The strange man's name was Alfred Wolfsohn. He was a forty-one-year-old voice teacher who, as a Jew, was not allowed to teach in Berlin. Charlotte had seen the Künstlerhilfe's letter of introduction for this flamboyant man who called himself "the prophet of song." Here was someone who perhaps thought even more highly of himself than Paula did of herself. Odd that he spent so much time at their apartment, and in Paula's music room.

Alfred Wolfsohn around 1932.

Surely it shouldn't take so long for Paula to evaluate his teaching qualifications.

Charlotte eavesdropped and heard Wolfsohn tell Paula that she used to sing more beautifully. Charlotte gradually understood that Wolfsohn wasn't there for Paula's approval so that he could get work coaching other singers. Instead, he had decided to transform Paula into the world's "greatest singer." He would be her redeemer, and perhaps her lover.

It was 1937, four years since Charlotte's exit from high school without getting a diploma. Now twenty, she had experienced the boredom of fashion school, followed by the exhilaration of art school. At least until she was denied her art prize. Now she could only paint there at night, which she continued to do. When she was at home, which was much of the time these days, there was no way *not* to hear Alfred Wolfsohn coaching Paula. They would usually begin at ten o'clock in the morning and work for hours. Wolfsohn told Paula that his techniques involved "going back to nature." They included wailing, screaming, even barking—not the usual vocal warm-up exercises of musical scales and études. They sounded like torture. Wolfsohn's musical theories were strange indeed.

One morning Wolfsohn arrived at his usual time, but Charlotte heard no piano, no singing. Instead, she heard Wolfsohn talking

Wolfsohn, as Charlotte painted him.

with Paula about his past. He described being buried alive under the bodies of dead soldiers at around age twenty—her age, she realized—during World War I and waking up among corpses. He talked about having depression and seizures after the war, and about seeing a psychiatrist who sent him to Italy to recover.

As Charlotte listened, he described not knowing who he was, and how he expected life to love him, because he had risen from the dead and survived. Instead, he learned that he needed to love life "in order to be this perfect creature whom you see before you." All this perplexed Charlotte. He was supposed to be a singing coach; instead he sounded like a madman. A few days later Charlotte heard him call Paula "my Madonna."

Madonna? Like the beautiful women Charlotte had seen in all those Italian masterpieces. Madonna? Charlotte put on her drab brown coat and came out of her room. In front of Wolfsohn, Paula told Charlotte that she looked dreadful, hands thrust deep into her pockets, hair not styled. Charlotte left, but not before she heard Wolfsohn ask Paula if Charlotte was her daughter.

"She's my husband's daughter, but I love her as if she were my own," Charlotte remembered Paula saying.

---

Alfred Wolfsohn confused twenty-year-old Charlotte. He spent a lot of time with Paula, adoring her, it seemed. And yet he had come to Christmas Eve dinner at the Salomons' with a young woman he called his fiancée. Charlotte tried to talk about him with Paula. She asked Paula how he could be in love with his fiancée when he was spending so much time at the Salomons' home. She also told Paula that she thought he was sensible, gifted, and a "noble specimen . . . of humanity." Paula explained that because he was so gifted, it was also fine to be crazy.

Despite her puzzlement, Charlotte found she could not stop thinking about Wolfsohn. She had learned to etch, and she spent hours at a time trying to make an etching of him that would show how much she liked him. She was convinced that she had a "profound subconscious fascination" for him. She portrayed him as a man standing by the sea. There was a group of people gathered around him, and they were listening to him speak. Behind them, in the distance, she included the figure of a solitary young man pointing toward his own head and making a "they're crazy" sign. As Charlotte carefully printed copies of the finished etching, her perfectionism got the best of her. "Even if it drives me out of my mind—I have to get it the way I want it," she wrote.

When she was at last satisfied with her work, Charlotte lurked in a park near her home where Wolfsohn often walked on his way to and from his coaching sessions with Paula. When Charlotte saw him, she said it was such luck, meeting like that. They settled together on a park bench that was technically off-limits for Jews. She gave him the etching and he said he would write to her with his opinion of it.

Charlotte was in Italy visiting her grandparents when Wolfsohn's letter arrived. She took the letter, her paints, and a sketchbook and went to a buttercup-strewn meadow under her favorite Italian-blue skies. When she read the letter, it seemed like a diagnosis. Wolfsohn began by saying that the etching "has no particular artistic merit and betrays no above-average

Wolfsohn and Paula at work.

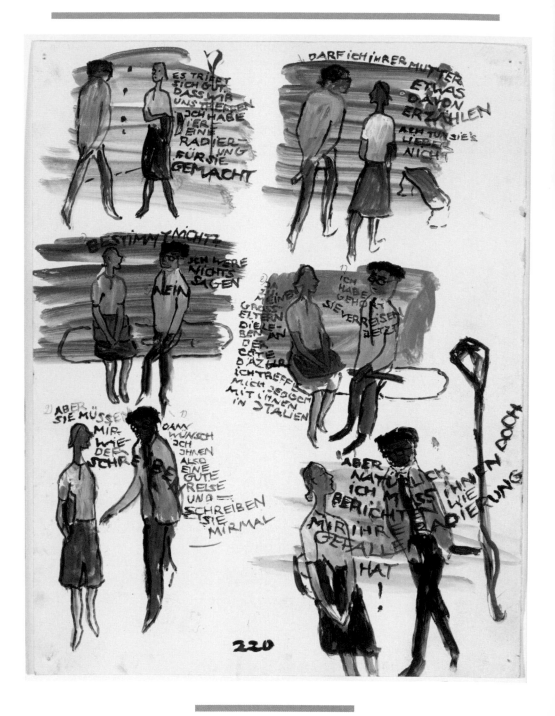

Charlotte and Wolfsohn in the park.

talent." Not encouraging. "But concept and execution reveal a touching effort." Somewhat better. She read on and came to the words "In my opinion you are destined to create something above average" (über den Durschnitt).

*Above average.*

As she thought about his words, she began to feel "elated" and "quite proud that someone finds it worth wasting his thoughts on her." Holding the folded letter on her lap, Charlotte made an impulsive, but important, artistic decision: she would make Wolfsohn's words come true. She would "create something *above average.*" Charlotte picked a four-leaf clover for Wolfsohn, for good luck.

When Charlotte returned to Berlin from Italy, she showed Wolfsohn nearly a dozen paintings. They were all part of her determination to create something above average. He sat at a table in Charlotte's bedroom and spread them out while she stood next to him in a dowdy blue dress, arms crossed, ankles crossed, eyes downcast.

Wolfsohn studied the pictures intensely, but briefly, before selecting two of them. One was called *The Meadow with the Yellow Buttercups*, painted with bright blues and greens. The second was titled *Death and the Maiden*, inspired by a Franz Schubert song, and was dark, with moody olive and gray tones. Charlotte told Wolfsohn he could have the buttercups, but he wanted both. He said *Death and the Maiden* was a painting of the two of them. Charlotte was the maiden, and he was Death because he had been buried alive. He folded his hands over the bottom edge of the painting and bent even closer to it, almost like he was praying.

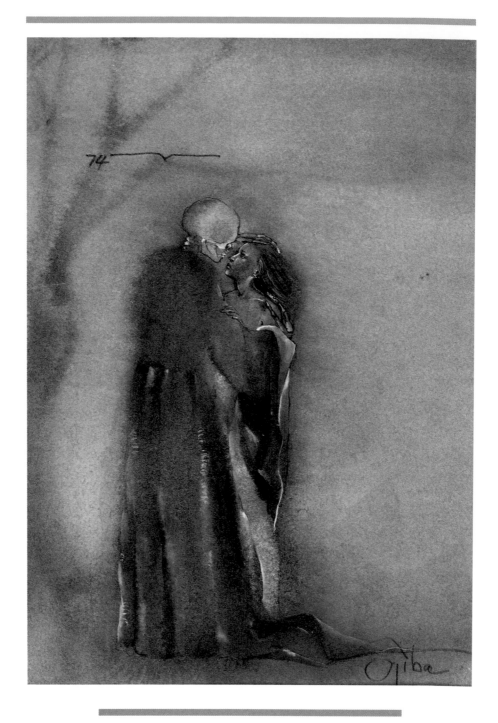

Charlotte's *Death and the Maiden* painting. (The word "Ojiba" in the
lower right corner was added later by one of Charlotte's students.)

Charlotte agreed to lend the second painting to him as he left her room to return to Paula's music room.

On one of his next trips to the Salomon home, Wolfsohn brought along one of his own manuscripts for Charlotte to illustrate. She thought it might be too hard for her, but he told her to try. He suggested they meet at the Station Café that evening so she could show him her first sketches. He said it was fine for young girls to go there. She was nearly twenty-one, yet still only a "young girl" in his mind.

When she arrived at the café, she found Wolfsohn seated at a table for two. He asked her to sit down but didn't do anything as courteous as pulling out her chair for her. He explained that he wanted her illustrations of his manuscript to be ready in time for his upcoming forty-second birthday on September 23, 1938. It was now March.

As Charlotte scowled at Wolfsohn, he started giving her advice. He told her she was too tense and needed to relax. He said not to cross her arms over her chest all the time, and that she should control her face so that people wouldn't know what she was thinking. Then he said she was pretty but that when she grimaced, she looked like an infant or a great-grandmother.

Charlotte listened, sometimes looking right at Wolfsohn, sometimes closing her eyes and hanging her head. He began describing his theories for teaching voice. The man could certainly talk. The longer he spoke, the more directly she gazed at him. He said she had adorable eyes, and not to be angry with him.

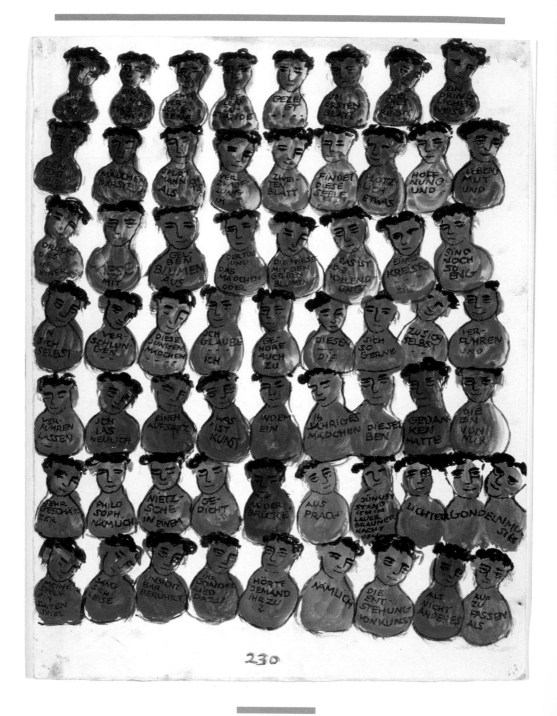

Wolfsohn, talking.

This made no sense to Charlotte. How in the world could she be angry with him? She was in love.

---

At the same time that she began to understand her own crush on Wolfsohn, Charlotte overheard him asking Paula to spend more time with him. One minute he was telling Charlotte she had adorable eyes, and the next minute she heard him obsessing over Paula's hands and saying how beautiful Paula was. Charlotte did not know what to make of this. Was she jealous?

She decided to tell Wolfsohn how she felt. With her art portfolio under her arm, she ambushed him from behind an advertising pillar on a street he often used. They went to the same café as last time, and before they even ordered drinks, he started telling her that he wanted them to be less formal around each other. This time he didn't call her a young lady; he called her a baby, and then he took her hand, and bowed his head. He said she had true painter's hands. So now it was her hands and not Paula's?

Charlotte said nothing at all about her feelings for him. She was only able to tell him that she wanted to paint his portrait, and he agreed.

---

Over the summer of 1938, Wolfsohn and Charlotte, now twenty-one, continued to meet often. Charlotte found that at times she wanted him to treat her like his sweetheart. At other times, he repulsed her. They would sneak kisses under lampposts in the street or snuggle together on off-limits park benches. He took

Charlotte and Wolfsohn embrace on an off-limits park bench.

Charlotte boating. And sometimes, when Paula and Albert went to a Kulturbund event in the evening, Wolfsohn showed up at the apartment. They kissed. They listened to music together on the gramophone. He talked about his work, his musical and philosophical theories, the next book he hoped to write.

As September approached, Charlotte was running out of time to complete the illustrations she had promised him for his birthday. She painted night and day to finish and thought the pictures "turned out surprisingly well." When she arrived at the café on his birthday, she saw that he had already finished his drink, and the empty plate in front of him held only a fork. He seemed rushed and impatient, telling her that he would look at his present later, that he didn't have time. She had just spent six months painting this gift for him, and now he didn't have time to even look?

Afterward, at home in her room, Charlotte stood by the open window "filled with grief mingled with rage." She began throwing money out the window, tossing coins, one by one. Then she rested her arms on the windowsill and stared out, and then down three floors, to the ground below. She could throw herself out too, she realized.

In the end, she decided Wolfsohn wasn't worth it. "Besides," she wrote, "some day I'll find out how he liked the illustrations."

Six weeks later, on the night of November 9, soldiers and citizens attacked Jewish people in Germany, Austria, and part of Czechoslovakia. This was called *Kristallnacht* (Night of Broken Glass) because of all the shattered windows in destroyed Jewish homes and businesses. Two days earlier, on November 7 in Paris,

Charlotte observes Hitler Youth looting Jewish shops.

a seventeen-year-old Polish Jewish refugee named Herschel Grynszpan had shot, and seriously wounded, Ernst vom Rath, a German embassy official. Vom Rath died on November 9 and the Nazis used his death as their pretext to support attacks on Jews.

Charlotte watched, shocked, as the family's frightened maid told Albert to hide, saying Jews were being arrested all over town. Charlotte looked at her father, hunched over his meal. He looked defeated. Paula encouraged him to flee to the Jewish hospital, where he might be safe. He took her advice but on November 10 he was arrested and sent to the Sachsenhausen concentration camp, about twenty miles north of Berlin, and forced into slave labor in the camp. He was one of thirty thousand Jewish men rounded up after *Kristallnacht* in parts of Germany, Austria, and Czechoslovakia.

Charlotte and Paula remained in the apartment, where Wolfsohn had "virtually taken up residence," as Charlotte later wrote. The maid thought this was very strange, and at times, Charlotte agreed. Wolfsohn ranted about seeing into the future. He talked about writing a new book, and worried about being arrested himself. Charlotte could hardly stand being at home, but there was nowhere else to go. "I've had enough of this life," she wrote, "I've had enough of these times."

But a determined Paula, with help from friends and acquaintances within the developing resistance movement, and using fake documents, was able to obtain release papers for her husband. "I learned to concentrate," Paula said. "I was running to this person and that person all day, forging dates on a release form, contacting colleagues in the underground, and with their

"Ich hab genug" (I've had enough).

help I got two people out—my husband and a lawyer who lived on our street."

Albert was freed in late November, and although weak and sick, he wasted no time in trying to protect Charlotte from what he had just been through.

## CHAPTER FIVE

# EXILED

*She was a sensitive young woman with*
*a deep artistic feeling.*
—Emil Straus, family friend

Many German Jews were in denial and thought the trouble with the Nazis would not last much longer, but after the terror of *Kristallnacht* and the Sachsenhausen camp, and fearing what lay ahead, Albert and Paula decided the family had to leave Germany.

Charlotte was first. In December 1938, several months before her twenty-second birthday, she stood on a platform at Berlin's cavernous Anhalter train station and said goodbye to Paula. Very hopeful he would see her again and weighing only ninety pounds after his time in the Sachsenhausen camp, her father did not come to see her off. Minutes before she boarded her train for France, Charlotte saw Wolfsohn hurrying down the platform to say goodbye. The night before, Charlotte had gone to Wolfsohn's apartment, where he told her never to forget that he believed in

Charlotte shortly before she left Berlin.

her. He also reminded her, as she wrote later, that "in order to love life completely, perhaps it is necessary to embrace and comprehend its other side: death."

Charlotte was headed for the village of Villefranche-sur-Mer in the South of France, near Nice, to live with her grand-parents, the Grun-walds. In the spring of 1934, after a stay in Rome,

Ottilie Moore and the Grunwalds around 1939.

her grandparents had chosen not to go home to the frightening situation in Germany. Instead, they had taken refuge in France with a wealthy friend, German American widow Ottilie Moore. Ottilie owned a property in Villefranche, called "L'Hermitage" (the Hermitage), where she welcomed refugees feeling from the Nazis, especially children. From early 1939 until fall 1941, she cared for over three hundred refugee children—according to her nephew—whose parents had been arrested or killed or had simply disappeared, sheltering them in small groups as they passed through her home on their way to safety.

Charlotte sat by herself on the train and stared out the window, her face expressionless. She was not required to have a passport until age twenty-two, which meant she could cross borders more easily than her parents. Weekend vacation passes were still allowed, so Paula told the authorities that Charlotte was going on a short visit to her grandparents. To facilitate the lie, Charlotte took very little luggage, but she managed to find room for three favorite recordings of Paula, a painting smock, and some art supplies. She also had letters with her falsely stating that her grandparents were ill and had no family nearby. Without these letters she might have been turned back at the French-German border.

Albert and Paula believed Charlotte would be safe with her grandparents in France until they could join her there. At first, Albert and Paula were correct in thinking they could make the trip too. Then their passports were confiscated, so they could not follow Charlotte to France as planned. Instead, in March 1939, only a few months after Charlotte left for France, Albert and Paula had an opportunity to flee to Amsterdam with forged passports. Later Paula explained their journey:

> We headed to Amsterdam because there we had Jewish friends and since we could only take handbags, no money, we needed friends. There was a German-Swedish man in the underground with me. . . . He got us false passports, then got on a plane with us, but we pretended not to know him. When we arrived in Amsterdam, he took the passports and went back on the next plane.

At first, Albert and Paula lived with Paula's friend from Berlin, the conductor Kurt Singer. He had also fled Germany and was no

Guest house at L'Hermitage.

longer conducting symphony orchestras and organizing concerts. Instead, he was giving music lessons in his home, where his students included Margot and Anne Frank.

The plan was for Albert and Paula to join Charlotte in France and then travel to the United States as a family. Albert, Paula, and Charlotte knew the physicist and Nobel Prize recipient Albert Einstein from Berlin, and Einstein had written a letter of support. The Metropolitan Opera in New York had written a letter of artistic support for Paula. Even so, the United States consulate in Rotterdam refused to grant them visas. Without passports or travel documents, their only choice was to remain in Amsterdam.

Charlotte was stranded in France.

---

The Grunwalds lived in a guest house on the grounds of Ottilie Moore's property, on a lush hillside in Villefranche. Once Charlotte arrived from Berlin, she moved in with the couple.

She loved the villa's luxurious walled garden and it made her feel safe. It was an oasis of olive and orange trees, colorful flowers, and shady pines. She began painting the garden's luminous sun-drenched vegetation, and she could see and paint the brilliant blues of the Mediterranean Sea in the distance. She painted rooftops overlooking the sea; an orchard outside the cottage; the beautiful villa. And sometimes she lay on her back for hours and studied the blue hues of the sky through the shimmering tree leaves. A family friend later described her as "renewed and clear, out of so much suffering and sorrow."

Living with her grandparents was a challenge. Charlotte spent all her time painting, and they did not approve. Grandmother asked her if she was "in the world only to paint." Grandfather said she should go out and find work as a housemaid, "like all the others," referring to other girls her age. For her grandparents, art was not a serious pursuit. For Charlotte, it was her world.

Except that her world was full of small children. She couldn't go anywhere in the garden without running into some of Ottilie's charges. She wished they wouldn't call out to her, "Bonjour,

Charlotte with her grandparents around 1939/40.

Lolotte." Each time they did this, Charlotte—always shy, even with children—turned away and blushed beet red. And when Ottilie scheduled events and activities for them, Charlotte hid. Ottilie's ten-year-old nephew Wally said Charlotte was "not of this world" and called her "the Mute." He said they heard Charlotte's voice only when she argued with her grandmother.

Although the children made her uncomfortable, throughout the spring and summer of 1939, Charlotte began to feel more relaxed around Ottilie. She was from New York City and the daughter of Adolf Gobel, a German American businessman who had made his fortune in the sausage industry. Charlotte observed that Ottilie "felt despair about life despite her immense financial resources. She had

Ottilie Moore's dining room at L'Hermitage, with
harlotte's paintings hanging on the walls.

a need for action, for satisfaction, for insatiable curiosity about life
itself and what it can offer." For Charlotte, Ottilie was also someone
who genuinely liked her art. "She was the only person who took
pleasure in my drawings," Charlotte wrote, "and so she bought
lots of them from me and hung them nicely framed in her house."
These sales gave Charlotte a boost of confidence, and some much-
appreciated income.

Charlotte also gave drawing lessons, as a paid professional
artist, to Ottilie's ten-year-old daughter, Didi. One day, Didi
tried to climb a tree in the garden at L'Hermitage on a dare from
Wally and became frightened. Once Didi was safely out of the
tree, Charlotte's advice to her was "Let's make a painting of it."

Together they drew a huge scary tree with scratchy branches but with a softness in the leaves. Charlotte knew that making art would help.

Eventually Charlotte managed to find adult friends. Emil Straus was Grandfather's French teacher at the Nice Centre Universitaire and was German like her. At first, she was very guarded around him. Then he told her he knew Paula from back in Germany, which interested Charlotte. Emil and his wife Hilde liked to talk about

Emil Straus.

painting and drawing and poetry and music, so Charlotte often visited them at their home in Nice. Emil described Charlotte around the time he met her:

> *Wherever she happened to be, she pulled out her sketchbook. She had to unburden herself, and her language was pencil or brush. . . . In company she was unsure of herself. She detested having to talk, and especially answering questions about herself. Her grandparents thought her stupid and sullen but that was not the case; she was a sensitive young woman with a deep artistic feeling and an intense emotional life. . . .*

*I discovered not only a profound lover of painting and music, but also an uncommonly intelligent and independent-minded young girl.*

Charlotte had found a refuge in Villefranche. But Ottilie's garden began to feel less safe when the news arrived that on September 1, 1939, the Nazis had invaded Poland. Two days later Britain and France declared war on Germany.

World War II had begun.

CHAPTER SIX

## STUNNED

*Joy, O joy, divinest spark*
—from Ludwig van Beethoven and
Friedrich Schiller's "Ode to Joy"

When war was declared in September, Grandmother reacted badly. Charlotte found her sitting in front of the radio, head down, arms tightly hugging her knees. Charlotte sat nearby, unsure what to do. Grandmother was listening to a broadcast about the war in Germany.

Her grandparents' fiftieth wedding anniversary was coming up on October 28, 1939. Charlotte painted a small booklet, "1889–1939: A little history in pictures from my grandmother's stories," as a gift. Charlotte added words to her paintings, so it was almost like a children's picture book. There were fifteen painted pages showing scenes of her grandparents being introduced, their courtship, their wedding, their two daughters,

Grandmother distraught in front of the radio, September 1939.

Pages from Charlotte's gift booklet for her grandparents' fiftieth wedding anniversary.

their travels. There was a picture of the couple with Ottilie Moore at L'Hermitage. In the final image Charlotte had painted herself wearing a lavender party dress and standing at a beautifully laid table with a wineglass in her right hand. She was toasting her grandparents, seated across from each other at the table. Charlotte hoped the little book would cheer up Grandmother and show her what a full and beautiful life she was living. The story ended with Charlotte's words, "Let art and nature help you overcome each difficulty."

Grandmother may have perked up slightly, but the relationship with Ottilie Moore was fraying. The Grunwalds had lived in her guest house for five years and accepted her generosity and kindness. Now Ottilie seemed preoccupied with a new friend, a man named Alexander Nagler. Like them, he was a refugee. Ottilie had hired him as a caretaker to help her with the children she had rescued.

Charlotte found him to be uninteresting and unmotivated. "He just wanted to get as much for himself as he could," she wrote, "from the passion of a slightly crazy, rich American woman."

Charlotte's grandparents worried that Ottilie was losing interest in them. They said terrible things about her behind her back, which upset Charlotte. Ottilie was her friend and supported her as an artist. "I couldn't bear living alongside my grandparents," Charlotte wrote, "as they took everything from this woman and at the same time hearing them say the meanest things about her."

Early in 1940, Charlotte and her grandparents moved to a small apartment in the town of Nice, five miles away from Ottilie's villa. Charlotte had no choice; her grandparents were the only family she had nearby. Ottilie must "have felt deeply disappointed by each of many people she had given a part of herself to," Charlotte wrote, "because almost everyone abandoned her the way my grandparents had done: with ingratitude, contempt, and scorn!" Charlotte still believed that Ottilie was her friend, and she had felt safe inside the high, strong garden walls at the villa. How could she possibly paint inside a small apartment with this bitter and depressed old couple?

One night in mid-March, Charlotte walked into the apartment's bathroom and was horrified to find Grandmother trying to hang herself. Charlotte lowered Grandmother to the floor as Grandfather walked in, relieved to find his wife was still alive. As Charlotte gently put her back into bed, Grandmother begged her husband and Charlotte to let her die. Charlotte decided then and there that she must protect and save her grandmother from ever trying anything like this again. Charlotte felt shocked and sick but determined.

Charlotte spent the next several days sitting on Grandmother's bed describing the rays of sunlight, the gorgeous flowers outside, the majestic mountains in the distance—anything to boost Grandmother's mood. She kept a sketchbook on her lap and drew Grandmother's face full of wrinkles and sadness. Charlotte had a beautiful voice, and she sang to Grandmother, the glorious "Ode to Joy" from Beethoven's Ninth Symphony.

Grandfather told Charlotte that her ideas, suggestions, and songs were *Quatsch* (nonsense). But Charlotte did not give up. Then he shocked Charlotte with the news that this was not the first time a member of her family had attempted suicide. Her Aunt Charlotte—the same Aunt Charlotte she had been named for—had drowned herself at age eighteen in a lake near Berlin. And Grandmother's brother Georg, a talented young lawyer, had also drowned himself. Grandmother's mother—Charlotte's great-grandmother—had tried to kill herself for eight years after Georg's death.

Charlotte listened in disbelief as Grandfather told her that her own mother, her cherished Franziska, had not died from the flu. Instead, she had tried, and failed, to poison herself. That must have been why her mother had been whisked away to the grandparents' apartment, Charlotte realized, and why there was always a nurse in the room when she and her father visited. In excruciating detail Grandfather told Charlotte that one day, when the nurse was out of the room for only a moment, Franziska threw herself out the window to her death. "I knew nothing of all that," Charlotte wrote.

For the past fourteen years Charlotte had been denied the truth about her own mother. Why had the people she loved and trusted—Paula, her father, her grandparents—not been honest with her?

Now Grandfather wouldn't stop talking. It seemed to Charlotte that he droned endlessly, almost boastfully, about all the suicides, the unhappiness, and the mental illness in her family. His words became a blur of other aunts, uncles, sisters, husbands, eight of her relatives in total. He even told Charlotte that her own parents had married against his wishes. This was too much sadness for Charlotte, with Grandmother dozing and lying depressed and broken-spirited on the bed in front of her.

***

Despite her own grief—and the shock of learning the truth about her past—Charlotte kept trying to help Grandmother. More songs. More descriptions of the painters' light and the artists' colors of the South of France. Charlotte thought again of Wolfsohn and how he said he believed in her, and she began to see signs of improvement. Grandmother rallied. She started agreeing with Charlotte. Exquisite light? Yes. Spectacular mountains? Yes. Reasons to live? Yes, and yes.

Charlotte, ever dutiful, continued to care for her grandmother. Thoughts of the family suicides cluttered her mind. She didn't have to be like her relatives, she told herself. Instead, she decided she would "live for them all." She encouraged Grandmother to write poetry again, something her grandmother had always loved and had talent for. In the good moments, Charlotte hoped Grandmother could recover completely.

Grandfather describes the family suicides.

In the bad moments, Charlotte felt her task and her life were impossible. So impossible, that on March 19, 1940, Charlotte vowed she would leave the following morning. She had been up all night with Grandmother for the last four or five nights. Grandmother was raving about her first daughter drowning, and then asking Charlotte to strangle Grandfather for her. The next morning, Charlotte told Grandfather that he was still alive thanks to her. She also suggested that he give Grandmother morphine as "an act of mercy." "I can't stand it any more," Charlotte wrote, "I have to leave them."

She never had the chance. Later that day, when Grandfather had gone out for a walk, Grandmother used the opportunity to throw herself out the window, just like Charlotte's own mother had done. Charlotte covered the corpse in the garden with a white bedsheet before Grandfather returned. When he did, carrying a bouquet of red carnations for his wife, he showed no real surprise that she had finally succeeded in killing herself. Charlotte wrote to her parents later saying that she had nearly been dragged through the window, too, while trying to stop Grandmother.

Charlotte's emotions confused and scared her. She was afraid she would go mad too. There was a suicide epidemic in her family. Would she be next? "My life began," she wrote, "when my grandmother wanted to take her life—when I came to know that my mother too had taken her life—just like her whole family—as I came to find out that—I, myself, am the only survivor and deep inside I felt the same predisposition[,] the tendency to desperation and toward death."

# CHAPTER SEVEN

## BROKEN

*I would not say Gurs was Auschwitz,*
*but it was what they called the little hell*
*before the big one.*
—Hanne Hirsch Liebmann,
Gurs internment camp survivor

Charlotte had very little time to think about her own mental stability, or Grandmother's death, or even to grieve for her own mother now that she knew the truth about the suicide. The insanity of the world she lived in was closing in on her.

On May 10, 1940, less than two months after Grandmother's death, France was invaded by Nazi Germany. Charlotte, who had just turned twenty-three, was now less safe. Like other German Jewish refugees, she and Grandfather were considered "enemy aliens" or possible spies or *indésirables*, "undesirables."

Two and a half weeks later, on May 27, Charlotte saw an *avis*, an official announcement, that changed things even more. It was printed in the local newspaper, *L'éclaireur de Nice*, and was pasted on walls around town in the form of large posters. The instructions were clear:

## LES FEMMES RESSORTISSANTES ALLEMANDES DOIVENT SE RENDRE AU CENTRE DE GURS.

(FEMALE GERMAN NATIONALS MUST REPORT TO THE GURS CENTER.)

The Gurs center?

As it turned out, Gurs was an internment camp in the Josbaig Valley at the foot of the Pyrénées Mountains in southwestern France, about five hundred miles west of Nice. Details in the police announcement said she had to be there before June 1—only five days away—or would be subject to arrest. She was limited to sixty-six pounds of baggage, including enough food for three days, along with silverware, a tin cup, and eating utensils. And she was required to travel at her own expense. Before she could leave, she first had to report to the local authorities at 8:00 a.m. on Wednesday the 29th to show her official paperwork. That didn't leave much time.

What would she do with Grandfather? He was seventy-eight years old and needed her help. She would have to take him with her to Gurs.

The Gurs camp, in the wet seasons, was like a muddy swamp, about 1.2 miles long and covering almost two hundred acres, surrounded by barbed-wire fence. There was one road, with row upon row of miserable, segregated male and female barracks on either side, made of thin wood with leaky tar-paper roofing. There were 382 barracks in total, enough to house twenty thousand internees. No trees, little green, mostly mud. Treacherous mud. One night, while trying to make her way to the toilets in the dark, a woman slipped, fell, and suffocated in the thick soupy muck. Some of the internees tried to use stones to create a pathway, but the mud was too deep. They strung up rope to help find the open-air toilets at night, but people fell anyway.

There were sixty women in a barrack that was roughly eighty feet long by twenty feet wide, which meant they each had about twenty-six square feet of space. With few windows and little indoor lighting—apart from some dim, bare lightbulbs—and no chairs or benches of any kind, it was hard to do much of anything. Thirty women shared one daily loaf of bread about eighteen inches long. One of the women internees was assigned to divide it, and fights broke out if the portions weren't torn equally. Other meager food rations included hard-to-digest bean or rice soup and a daily sardine or minuscule piece of meat. The women slept on damp, dirty straw-filled sacks thrown on the floor, in the company of rats. The water was undrinkable and the only place to bathe was at outdoor faucets, while the camp guards watched. The toilets looked like animal troughs. Gurs was no better than a sewer. Hundreds of people died there from diseases like dysentery and typhoid.

Charlotte never wrote about the Gurs camp, nor did she paint it, but she did write about traveling to the area. She and Grandfather made the trip "in a railway car crammed with thousands of totally exhausted people." She compared that journey to being on her own with Grandfather. "I'd rather have ten more nights like this than a single one alone with him." Charlotte sketched what she

Gurs internment camp.

saw in the train: a couple with a baby, Grandfather looking tired and frustrated, groups of people trying to sleep.

It is not known exactly how long they stayed in the Gurs region or what their experience was, but Charlotte was required to report there, and she believed in following rules. She and Grandfather would have arrived around June 1 in a wave of people from throughout France, and likely remained in the area for three weeks. With this deluge of arrivals, the camp was pressed for space. Some people were sent to the barracks; others were housed in tents in a nearby sports stadium. On Monday, June 24, the Gurs camp director, Commandant Davergne, a Frenchman, instructed several of the women internees to burn the occupancy lists. "Ça fait un bon feu de joie," wrote the son of a camp survivor (It makes a good

Charlotte and Grandfather on a train to the Pyrénées.

fire of joy). Davergne did this to protect the identities of hundreds of individuals from the Nazis, possibly including Charlotte and Grandfather, but it remains impossible to prove or disprove their internment. The commandant then allowed anyone to leave who wished to and had somewhere to go. Davergne himself left Gurs the following November and became active in the French Resistance.

Charlotte's father later wrote that after speaking with people in Nice, he did not believe Charlotte and her grandfather had been interned. As well as the journey to the Pyrénées with Grandfather, Charlotte also wrote and painted about her return to Nice. While she was trying to book a train back to Nice, they had to find somewhere to stay. Grandfather felt it was perfectly fine to share a bed somewhere. Charlotte disagreed; she wanted her own hotel room. She tried telling Grandfather how beautiful the Pyrénées Mountains were but he only wanted to find lodging. She told the hotel keeper that she couldn't sleep next to her grandfather and asked if it was possible to sleep somewhere else. The woman found her a separate room. "To sleep again after three weeks!" she later wrote. This could suggest that they were in the group released on June 24 by Commandant Davergne, having arrived, by law, no later than June 1.

At the hotel, Charlotte met another German refugee, who told her he had left his belongings in a nearby forest while he searched for his lost family. He thought his oldest daughter might still be in the Gurs camp. He had no idea where his wife and other child were. Charlotte tried to sympathize. Then he put his arm around her and held her hand, which made her uncomfortable. That night, she barricaded herself in her room, pushing chairs and a

"Go ahead and kill yourself."

table in front of the door. The man managed to get in through the window and she screamed for help. The hotel owner told him to leave. What was this war doing to people?

In spite of the difficulties, the beauty of the Pyrénées Mountains was not lost on Charlotte. "God[,] my God[,] oh is that beautiful," she wrote. Once she was able to book a return train, she remembered telling Grandfather, "I have a feeling the whole world has to be put together again." Just like when she had tried to encourage Grandmother, he again called Charlotte's thoughts nonsense. He told her to go ahead and kill herself so that he wouldn't be plagued by her annoying chatter. Leaving the Gurs area when they did probably saved their lives. Over the next several years Gurs was used as an intermediate stop for thousands of Jews being sent to Nazi death camps in Poland.

After their return to the Nice apartment, the relationship between Charlotte and Grandfather remained stressed. They often went for days without speaking to each other. Charlotte was badly upset by her time in the Pyrénées. "I saw the whole world fall apart before my eyes," she wrote. "I saw it turn to chaos." She still hadn't had much opportunity to process the new knowledge of all the suicide deaths in her family. When would it be her turn? Even Grandfather seemed to think that her own suicide would be welcome. And now the insanity of the war was increasing. She had been able to exchange letters with her father and Paula in Amsterdam, but the Nazis had also invaded the Netherlands and Belgium in early May and mail had been cut off. The city of Nice had been a refuge for Jews trying to escape the Nazis, but how long would that last?

Odette and Georges Moridis, October 1940.

Charlotte was despondent. Her life looked like a long, endless wave of death, separation, fear, and denial. "I believed strongly," she wrote, "that this war would mean a deluge, it would become clear finally that humankind, culture and education are laughable notions constructed by humanity to be destroyed with thoughtless wild force, by humankind itself." Her fights with Grandfather intensified, and he became even more psychologically abusive. He criticized her. He belittled her. He took too much of her time. "[I] was desperately unhappy," she wrote. "I was tied to my grandfather, a play-actor—and an optimistic one at that—without a backdrop. Not a bad person as such, just like most everyone. A shallow type. . . . He was someone who had never felt true passion for anything."

The family's doctor and friend in Villefranche, Dr. Georges Moridis, helped Charlotte in the best possible way: he told her to return to her painting. This made complete sense to Charlotte.

Self-portrait, 1940.

She created a self-portrait, possibly based on a photograph someone had taken of her. She painted her usually wild, unruly hair combed back and away from her face in a severe style, with her head only partially turned toward the viewer. She painted a facial expression that made her look wary and untrusting. The white paint she used for her eyes was so bright that an observer would feel sucked right into them.

"My love of drawing grew and grew," she wrote, "the more I experienced it as a blessed act." She painted the sea. She painted rooftops. Landscapes. Portraits. She remembered her own advice to Grandmother, that instead of taking her life, Grandmother could use that same power to describe it through her poetry. This made

Charlotte think about her beloved Wolfsohn. He had once said that "one must first go into oneself to be able to go out of oneself."

"I had to go deeper into solitude," she wrote; "then maybe I could find—what I had to find! It is my *self*: a name for myself."

## CHAPTER EIGHT

# OBSESSED

*She was very introverted. And very*
*unhappy. She was never cheerful, no. . . .*
*She was a quiet girl. She never went*
*out with other young people.*

—Ottilie Moore describing Charlotte

For about a year after her return from the Pyrénées, Charlotte is thought to have lived mostly in Nice, taking care of Grandfather. Northern and western France had become an "Occupied Zone," governed by Germany. Southern and parts of eastern France were an "Unoccupied Zone," but under Nazi-approved French control. "We lived seemingly peaceful lives on the Côte d'Azure," Charlotte wrote. But she was feeling "crushed by the proximity of [her] grandfather" as the world "fell ever more apart." She found herself struggling with the idea of "whether to commit suicide or to undertake something totally, wildly special."

Special won. "In the presence of the scorching sun, purple sea, and luxuriant blossoms," she wrote, "the memory of an experience . . . came back." The memory was of Wolfsohn. She still "loved him as much as ever." He had told her that "in order to love life still more, one should once have died" as he had done when he was left for dead in the trenches of World War I. Living with Grandfather was like dying. She felt that she had "to vanish for a while from the human plane and make every sacrifice in order to create."

Help came from her friend Ottilie Moore, who thought Charlotte was an artistic genius. High praise, since Ottilie was a collector of fine art. Just like Dr. Moridis, Ottilie encouraged Charlotte to paint her way out of her depression. "I said that, if there is something inside you, it has to come out. Then you also have to help get it out," Ottilie said later.

Ottilie understood how oppressive Grandfather's presence was for Charlotte so she invited him back to L'Hermitage later in 1940 so that Charlotte could stay in the Nice apartment and paint. She was exploring a new idea about painting her own life story. But once Grandfather was back at Ottilie's villa he misbehaved. He stole fruit and blamed the children in Ottilie's care. He criticized Ottilie in front of the servants. Ottilie had no choice but to send him back to Charlotte.

In Grandfather's presence, Charlotte felt her despair and discouragement return. Ottilie stepped in again and invited Charlotte back to L'Hermitage for several months in the summer of 1941 to continue painting her life. "The war raged on," Charlotte wrote, "and I sat there by the sea and looked deep into the heart of humanity."

Her art supplies were limited but she had notebook-sized watercolor paper (ten inches by thirteen inches), tracing paper, paintbrushes, and tubes of red, blue, yellow, and white gouache (nontransparent watercolor paint). With the three primary colors and a bit of white, she could make any other color she wanted.

Charlotte stared at the paper in front of her and thought about her past. A play. About her life. She was writing and painting a play. Songs floated through her head. Music. There would be music in her play.

A play was composed of acts and scenes. Charlotte squeezed out some blue paint and added a little red paint to make a deeper blue. She painted act 1, scene 1: Aunt Charlotte walking down the stairway inside her parents' home, out into the dark night, toward a bleak, murky lake. "1913 One November day," she wrote, "[Aunt] Charlotte . . . left her parents' home and threw herself into the water." Charlotte Salomon's "totally wildly special" creation was well underway. She was creating her masterpiece.

Charlotte's brushstrokes were often bold and swirling. At other times they looked like delicate embroidery stitches. She used this stitch technique in an act 1 painting of the nursery in her Berlin apartment to show details in her crib and ruffly blankets. When she reached act 1, scene 5, she applied the same stitch-like brushstrokes again to paint the clothing she wore as a child, standing uncomfortably with her parents, Franziska and Albert. They looked connected; but she painted her child self separate and distant, as if walking off the page.

Charlotte as a child, with her parents.

Just a few pages later, she showed her mother, sad and lonely. Charlotte painted the words, "Thus she would stand and stand at the window—yearning and dreaming." She often painted the theme of suicide related to windows. But in another scene, she painted herself standing at that hotel window in the Pyrénées and announcing optimistically, "Gott mein Gott O ist das Schön" (God[,] my God[,] oh is that beautiful).

Charlotte looked at her stack of several hundred blank tracing-paper sheets. Sliding one on top of her brightly painted pages made the tracing paper look like a curtain or a veil or, better yet, a theatrical scrim (a translucent theater curtain). Charlotte placed one on top of a painting from act 1. The figure underneath the tracing paper was Franziska, her mother. She taped the tracing

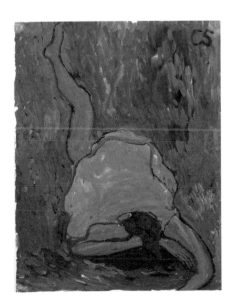 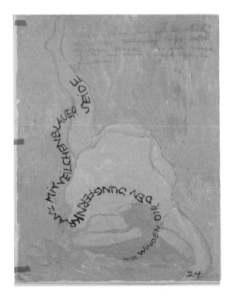

Painting of Franziska (left). The same painting with its overlay (right).

paper to the painting along the left edge. Then she painted German words on the tracing paper in capital letters, following the contours of her mother's corpse.

With the tracing-paper "screens" in place, her paintings looked like dreams or memories or nightmares. She did this for painting after painting—over three hundred times—until most of her tracing paper was probably gone. Then she began painting words directly onto the surfaces of the pictures—still using all capital letters—and her words became part of the art. In a scene where Grandfather described family suicide after family suicide to her, she painted his head sixty-three times over five pages and crowded the blank space around him with his echoing words. *Your mother . . . Aunt Charlotte . . . Grandma's brother . . . her nephew . . .* She painted the words in the same ultramarine that she used for his piercing, icy blue eyes.

She used the same colors repeatedly, for specific reasons, such as mixing red and yellow to make a sickly orange for paintings that expressed the fear and madness of the war. When she showed her father doing slave labor in a concentration camp, she painted the guard's uniform that same dirty orange to create a vicious, brutal feeling. When she painted a sea of Nazi soldiers marching in Berlin, she again used dark, muddy oranges for the soldiers' uniforms, mixed from red and yellow. And she chose to paint them without facial expressions.

When she created one of Paula's triumphant concert performances Charlotte used reds, blues, and golds to paint streaks and splashes of music as it poured from a symphony orchestra toward the audience. Later she painted one of Paula's final concerts. This

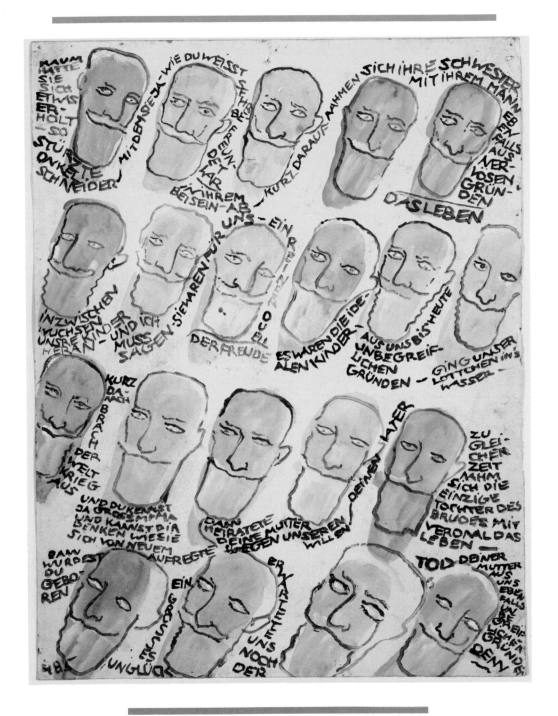

Grandfather talks endlessly about the suicides in Charlotte's family.

"Are you here in the world only to paint?"

time there were no glorious color splashes. Instead, Charlotte selected dark blue for the bullying words *Aus, Raus, Aus, Raus,* and underlined *Aus* in blood-red paint.

She depicted herself and her grandparents in Ottilie's garden in soft pastel South-of-France colors to convey the safe, idyllic Mediterranean coast. But then she added ominous dark-blue words to anchor the bottom of the picture:

GRANDMOTHER: *"ARE YOU HERE IN THE WORLD ONLY TO PAINT?"*

GRANDFATHER: *"YOU ARE MUCH TOO LENIENT WITH HER. WHY SHOULDN'T SHE WORK AS A HOUSEMAID, LIKE ALL THE OTHERS?"*

There were influences in Charlotte's art from painters such as Henri Matisse, Marc Chagall, and Vincent van Gogh, among many others. Like these artists, she created angular faces and curved bodies. She distorted shapes. She even used similar colors in similar ways. Like Matisse, she painted people with rounded shoulders, and used vivid reds and bright blues. She had studied the work of other artists while in art school in Berlin and is thought to have spent a week in Paris on her way to Villefranche and may have attended galleries and museums there. Her father had an art collection and art books in their home, and she could probably study the art in Ottilie's collection at L'Hermitage.

Somewhere along her creative path, Charlotte decided that her play needed a title, and a program. She painted a cover page with a red heart at the top. Then she placed her initials, CS, entwined and painted in blue under the title, *Leben? oder Theater? (Life? or Theater?)*. She added one gold and one dark blue circle around her swirled initials, almost like a bull's-eye. Surrounding the gold and blue circles were the words *Ein Singespiel*, painted in ruby red. Charlotte either misspelled the word *Singspiel* (song-play) or perhaps meant to make a pun with *song-game*. She painted DEDICATED TO OTTILIE MOORE in red capital letters on the top right-hand side of the next page. On the page after that, she labeled her work a "three-color musical play."

She painted a cast list of people from her own life. Aunt Charlotte, her mother Franziska, and Charlotte herself kept their real first names. She made up names for everyone else. She called her father Doktor Kann, the capable doctor. Paula became Paulinka BimBam, like a musical sound. Her grandparents were Herr und Frau Knarre, the creaky ones. And Wolfsohn became Amadeus—from Wolfgang Amadeus Mozart's name—and last name Daberlohn, perhaps suggesting a "penniless scrounger." "I was all the characters in my play," she wrote. "I learned to walk all their paths and became myself."

Charlotte painted program notes to describe her purpose. "The creation of the following paintings," she wrote, "is to be imagined as follows: A person is sitting beside the sea. She is painting. A tune suddenly enters her mind. As she starts to hum it, she notices that the tune exactly matches what she is trying to commit to paper. A text forms in her head, and she starts to sing the tune, with her own words, over and over again in a loud voice until the painting seems complete." It was as though a movie and its soundtrack were playing in Charlotte's mind.

But Charlotte's permit to stay in France—renewable every three months—required her to continue caring for Grandfather.

He had been sending her letters. They were mean. They were threatening. They reminded her of how paralyzed she felt in his presence. "The police would not allow me to stay away for long," she wrote. "My happiness was at an end. Absolutely at an end from brilliant sunlight into gray darkness." She had to return to Nice and Grandfather, "playing his 'theater of civilized, cultured men.'"

---

On September 22, 1941, Ottilie Moore left Villefranche for the United States with her daughter Didi, her nephew Wally, a large black poodle named Martini, and eight other refugee children—six were Jewish—whom she was able to include in her visa. She left behind at L'Hermitage two French and two Belgian children, and their Austrian caretaker, Alexander Nagler, Ottilie's presumed former lover.

Perhaps Ottilie thought Charlotte would be safe with Grandfather and Alexander, or perhaps it was impossible to get her an adult visa. When Ottilie's visa request to take the six children with her was approved in August, the US consulate in Nice was receiving two hundred to three hundred requests a day. The few that were approved went to "eminent intellectuals," not to regular German Jewish refugees. There is no evidence that Charlotte ever applied for a visa herself. The process was complex, and in addition to a visa to enter the United States, she would also have needed a visa to leave France, and two more to cross through Spain and then Portugal.

Ottilie was a celebrity in New York City because of her wealthy family, and she was interviewed by a journalist from the *New York*

Hôtel Belle Aurore, Saint-Jean-Cap-Ferrat, France, around 1938.

*Post* newspaper almost as soon as she and the children stepped off the SS *Excalibur* ocean liner on October 20, 1941, after their ten-day sail across the Atlantic. The children were from five countries: Austria, Britain, France, Poland, and the United States. They ranged from only a year old to age fifteen. Ottilie told the reporter about their escape, packed into a station wagon, and pulling a trailer with their luggage. She drove through France, Spain, and Portugal. They had several breakdowns because of poor-quality gasoline. Ottilie had traded a pig and twelve chickens with a neighbor in order to get the terrible gas in the first place. The day they sailed from Lisbon, Portugal, a Nazi bomber circled their ship. A British and a Portuguese ship were sunk nearby later that day. Ottilie also told the reporter that she planned to bring over four more refugees who were still at her home in France.

Sometime after Ottilie's departure, Charlotte moved to a small hotel called La Belle Aurore (Beautiful Dawn), six and a half miles southeast of Nice—and Grandfather—in the seaside resort town of Saint-Jean-Cap-Ferrat. Ottilie may have arranged for Alexander to pay for her room, and he also may have helped with Grandfather's care. Days of uninterrupted painting lifted Charlotte's spirits and her mood. But she took a big chance by leaving Grandfather because her permission to live freely in France—and not be arrested and sent back to the Pyrénées, or worse—required her to care for him.

She was obsessed with painting. She stayed in pink-carpeted room 1, and hardly stopped to eat or sleep. "Charlotte was a sunny girl," said the owner of La Belle Aurore, Marthe Pécher. "She had something clear, sincere, I would say almost luminous about her. I never noticed any timidity. In any case she did not seem timid with me and why should she? We were living, both of us, through some very bad moments. . . . Charlotte

Marthe Pécher around 1941.

rented only the room, she did not take meals, so sometimes in the evening I used to take her a bowl of hot soup—rutabaga, that horrible rutabaga—practically our only nourishment at the time."

Charlotte continued to paint obsessively at La Belle Aurore, even with Ottilie gone. She sang and hummed as she created. "She painted all the time," said Marthe, "always while humming." Sometimes she wrote in rhyme, which made her words sound even more musical. She selected popular musical tunes for her words to be sung to and she painted these indications on the backs of the pages or on the tracing-paper overlays or directly onto the paintings. Her musical references included passages from Georges Bizet's opera *Carmen*, works by Johann Sebastian Bach, and traditional German folksongs. Some were songs she remembered hearing Paula perform. She included the French and German national anthems, even a Nazi song. She spent entire days painting at La Belle Aurore, trying to make artistic sense of her life and the world around her.

Charlotte most likely painted in room 1 from sometime in the winter of 1941–42 until she finished *Life? or Theater?* in August 1942. Every hotel had a "police book" where each guest's stay was recorded but Marthe's *livre de police* is nowhere to be found. Charlotte told Marthe that she was painting her life, and Marthe remembered always seeing a different painting on Charlotte's drawing board. *Life? or Theater?* became an artistic retelling of her own life, a painted memoir. There were scenes from her parents' marriage, her childhood in Berlin, outings with Hase, Italian travels with her grandparents, art school, even the detestable fashion school. And Wolfsohn. She painted Wolfsohn in over 450 scenes. She expressed her feelings of powerlessness against events in her life, and against wartime madness. As her memoir progressed, her art became darker and sadder—but at the same time, her fear of self-destruction from her family's suicidal history, and her fear of destruction from the world around her, led to self-discovery.

"I left loneliness behind," she wrote, "with the feeling I had something I would be able to say to humanity."

## CHAPTER NINE

# POISONED

*The world needs people who say new things.*
—Charlotte Salomon, quoting Alfred Wolfsohn

While staying at La Belle Aurore, Charlotte learned that Jews—both French and foreign—needed to present themselves to the authorities. This was most likely the August 26, 1942, *rafle des Juifs étrangers* (roundup of foreign Jews) in the Nice region. Charlotte would have been twenty-five and, even after the Pyrénées, still believed in doing what was required, so she went. Marthe Pécher, who had not known Charlotte was Jewish, asked her why she had deliberately revealed herself. Charlotte answered, "I thought it was correct to present myself." She told Marthe that she was immediately put on a bus that was full and ready to depart for some unknown destination. Charlotte had no idea why, but at the last minute a police officer motioned for her to get off the bus. Charlotte said he told her to "leave right away, leave fast and don't come back, stay at home."

The people on that bus were headed for death camps in Poland. Unknown to them and the rest of the world, in January of 1942, Adolf Hitler's government had decided upon a "final solution" for the Jews: evacuation to death camps. A secret document from a secret conference outlined the procedure: "Europe is to be combed through from West to East in the course of the practical implementation of the final solution. . . . In occupied and unoccupied France the rounding up of the Jews for evacuation will, in all probability, be carried out without great difficulties."

Charlotte had no time to waste. The bus incident had shown her the danger. She had to finish *Life? or Theater?* She had to tell her life story. "I had to complete it!" she wrote. "No matter what the cost. What do I care about the police [or] Grandfather." She was rushing to finish.

She no longer added musical cues to her pictures and there were very few tracing-paper overlays. She had stopped painting pages full of tiny movie-like frames or sequences that looked like comic books. Her brushstrokes became faster, more sweeping. Buildings were often sketchier and backgrounds less complete. She painted nine of the last ten pages of *Life? or Theater?* in capital letters only, filling each page. First, she used red and blue, then purple made from combining them. Gradually she added yellow, and the letters became green and gold and orange and turquoise, then several lines of solid crimson. This was where she wrote about Wolfsohn and her decision not to commit suicide. She described showing him her *Death and the Maiden* painting back in Berlin and his response that it represented the two of them.

Charlotte begins *Life? or Theater?*

"If he was Death," she wrote, "then everything was all right." She did not have to kill herself like her ancestors.

For the play's final scene, Charlotte made a picture of herself, sitting by the sea, beginning a new painting. She drew herself seated with her legs folded under her, filling almost the entire page. She chose electric blue for the sea and sky in the distance and forest green for her swimsuit. On her bare tanned back, in her same bold capital letters, she painted the words LEBEN ODER THEATER (Life or Theater), without the question marks. Her right hand held a long-handled paintbrush and the drawing board on her lap was transparent, with the blue of the sea shimmering through it. She added her signature, CS, in a final painted arc at the bottom left. Charlotte had come full circle, painting herself beginning to paint her masterpiece as the ending of her musical play.

In about two years, in her race against the Nazis, Charlotte had made around thirteen hundred paintings—including the overlays—illustrating her life story. When she ran low on paper, she rejected some of the finished paintings, taping over the eyes and mouths of the characters, and painted new scenes on the reverse sides. The text for her painted memoir was around thirty-three thousand words long, enough for a novel. She selected over a thousand of her paintings and overlay sheets and organized them in her preferred order. She numbered the paintings, in blue paint, on the overlays or at the bottom center of each page.

During her productive time at La Belle Aurore, as Charlotte painted wildly to finish her masterpiece, her obligation to take care of Grandfather continued to haunt her. Her permit depended on it, and she knew she had to worry about the police. In the fall of 1942, she moved back into the Nice apartment. Grandfather was eighty years old and Charlotte continued to feel numb and dead around him. "The more that time passed," she wrote, "—the more I noticed—the old dullness starting to take hold of me again." She also worried that Grandfather would not be able to protect her from "Hitler's violent actions."

In February 1943, Grandfather died. His death certificate and eyewitness accounts stated that he collapsed in the street and died in the Nice apartment. But in a painted letter to Wolfsohn— using those same loud capital letters she had used throughout *Life? or Theater?*—Charlotte confessed to something darker. She had not heard from Wolfsohn since she last saw him in Berlin, over four years earlier, on the train platform the day she left. "Beloved friend," she began, "I thank you the way I love you as no one has ever loved another—the way I thank you no one has ever thanked another. You gave me courage and energy to come alive." Charlotte poured her heart out to Wolfsohn in thirty-five painted pages. "An incredible will to live at any cost was hidden inside me." She rushed her brushstrokes, left out punctuation, and often wrote in sentence fragments. Her words ran together and sometimes tilted downhill at the end of a line. "You said I was talented," she wrote, "even though the whole world insisted the opposite."

In the letter, using her same red, yellow, and blue gouache paints, she described the horror of living with her grandfather, the anguish of learning about all of the suicides in her family, the terror of living on the French Riviera under Hitler, and the help and friendship of Ottilie Moore. She told Wolfsohn that her letter's purpose was to make a confession. She had made Grandfather's omelet, and she had also made a decision. She knew where the container she needed was kept. Her grandparents had brought it with them from Germany, just in case. She picked it up and put some of the contents into Grandfather's omelet. As the drug began to work, Charlotte sat by Grandfather's bed and sketched him.

"Maybe by now he is already dead," she wrote. "Forgive me. A great deal of strength was needed for this, and it was all the strength left to me from the summer of Life and Theater! . . . As grandfather already fell asleep gently by intoxication with the 'Veronalomelette,' . . . it felt to me as though a voice called out: Theater is dead!"

Had eating the omelet caused Grandfather's death? Or had it simply weakened an already sick, sad, and disillusioned old man? Was Charlotte trying to help her grandfather at a time when assisted suicide was as shaming as *Selbstmord* (suicide)? Perhaps she was thinking about the night before Grandmother's death when she "tore my grandmother away from my softly snoring grandfather's neck—she definitely wanted to strangle him." Or was she simply trying to free herself from abuse and pain in order to make art?

## CHAPTER TEN

# MURDERED

*The more I saw how—humanity was disposed—*
*the more satisfaction I felt in drawing and in*
*any uninterrupted work.*
—Charlotte Salomon

After Grandfather's death, Charlotte—now almost twenty-six—moved back to L'Hermitage. "Mrs. Moore left me a friend," she wrote. "I didn't quite know what to do with him." She meant Alexander Nagler. Charlotte had been suspicious of him when he first arrived at L'Hermitage in March 1939, only a month or two after she joined her grandparents there. Alexander's sister-in-law Annie Nagler, who lived in the area and became friends with Charlotte, described Alexander as a "gentle and loyal man." But Annie's other observations were less favorable:

> When Madame Moore threw him out, he came back. Out, back—anyone could see how weak Alexander was. He lacked

*energy. He lacked French. . . . An accident in childhood
damaged his ear and hair. He had a terrible complex about
his scar. . . . Not very smart, not very apt. And he drank.*

In spite of his failings, Charlotte and Alexander had become
friends over the past four years. She could hardly avoid running into
him when she was living with her grandparents at L'Hermitage.
When Alexander became ill with stomach ulcers that required
surgery Charlotte decided to take care of him until he recovered.
"We were somewhat close," she wrote, "and I knew that he was
all alone[,] pretty weak in character and not surrounded by
friends—because everyone envied him for having in his hands
the management of the beautiful property." Charlotte was ready
to love someone again and felt she could be helpful to Alexander.
"I had the desire to love—just to have one person—I believed
I could be of use to," she wrote. She helped him with the four
remaining children at L'Hermitage and did the grocery shopping
because, unlike Alexander, she didn't lack French.

By the spring of 1943, conditions in the South of France had
become more dangerous. The previous November, Germany had
taken direct control of most of the French-controlled "Unoccupied
Zone." Also in November, the Italian army, which was allied with
Nazi Germany, had occupied the southeastern corner of France,
including Nice and its surroundings, but the Italians did not
enforce anti-Jewish policies very seriously. The greater fear was
that Germany would take over the entire region. Charlotte and
Alexander relied on each other and on trusted friends like Emil
and Hilde Straus, and Georges and Odette Moridis, to keep going.

Alexander Nagler around 1938.

Anti-Jewish feelings increased in the region, and the chance of betrayal grew. "How gruesome our existence had become," Charlotte wrote, "everything that a normal person—what gets called normal— would consider normal, it all gets destroyed by the cynical ridiculing laughter of a blood-drenched and self-destructive war-making humanity." The remaining children in Alexander's care at L'Hermitage were reclaimed by their families. Food was scarce and expensive on the black market. Alexander and Charlotte were alone at L'Hermitage, trying to stay away from the authorities. They grew closer. Emil Straus described Charlotte and Alexander's relationship:

> In these chaotic, uncertain times, he gave her a sense of
> security. They were living alone in the big house and he
> was almost the only human being with whom Charlotte
> could speak. . . . Nagler and Charlotte became dependent
> on each other; he was her companion, protector, and
> friend. . . . She had made up her mind to become his wife,
> but while her grandfather was alive she had been unable to
> gain his consent. . . . But Alexander Nagler and Charlotte
> loved each other.

Four months after Grandfather's death, on June 17, 1943, Charlotte married Alexander. She was twenty-six; he was thirty-eight. Their friends Odette and Georges Moridis were their witnesses. Against the advice of Dr. Moridis, who was working unofficially for the Resistance, Charlotte and Alexander filled out an official marriage registration and their latest personal information was recorded with the authorities, making them all too visible. Alexander listed himself as the

Charlotte's painting of Alexander.

director of a children's home. Charlotte's listing was *sans profession* (without a profession). It should have read *artiste et peintre* (artist and painter).

By mid-1943 there was talk of escape and rescue through Italy for the Jews in the Nice area. Angelo Donati, an Italian Jewish banker, diplomat, and philanthropist who lived in Nice, had begun piecing together a plan. He negotiated with the Italian foreign ministry to help thirty thousand French and German Jewish refugees in the South of France. They would travel to Italy and on from there to North Africa by sea. Donati worked to get money for his plan from the United States and from Britain. Both countries stalled. Italy had four passenger ships ready. Charlotte and Alexander, along with other Jews in the area, would certainly have heard of the Donati plan. So many Jews there knew Donati, and considered him their only possible way out, that in summer 1943 newborns were often named Angelo.

But the mass rescue failed. Italy surrendered to Germany in September 1943 and the Germans occupied the Italian zone, including Nice. They arrested every Jew they could find. They were even told to arrest people who simply looked Jewish based on racist stereotypes. For the authorities, this meant people with curly dark hair or a hooked nose or drooping eyelids.

At some point in 1943, Charlotte and Alexander wrapped *Life? or Theater?* into several packages. Charlotte slipped in her painted confession letter to Wolfsohn. The mail had been cut off for months, and she had not been able to send it, if she had even meant to. Alexander wrote *Property of Mrs. Moore* on the outer wrapper, hoping to protect the paintings. Charlotte, either alone or with Alexander, delivered the parcels to Dr. Moridis, and she is thought to have told him, "Keep this safe. It is my whole life. [C'est toute ma vie.]"

As the Nazis closed in, Charlotte and Alexander may have had choices. Marthe Pécher had a secret apartment in Nice. Dr. Moridis offered them a place to hide in the city-state of Monaco, ten miles east toward Italy. Emil Straus hid in the French Alps. Annie Nagler escaped on foot. But Charlotte and Alexander remained at L'Hermitage, where Charlotte had always felt safe. The couple probably did not know that back in April an arrest warrant had been issued for "the Jew Nagler."

The Drancy Transit Camp.

Three months after their marriage, on September 22, 1943, the German Gestapo (the Nazi secret police) found Charlotte and Alexander hiding in one of the outbuildings at L'Hermitage. They arrested all three of them. Three, because Charlotte was pregnant. Ottilie's loyal housekeeper, Vittoria Bravi, reported hearing truck doors slamming, followed by Charlotte's screams. Inside Ottilie's villa with its secure garden walls, she had felt safe. But outside, those walls were covered with graffiti like *A bas les juifs* (Down with Jews). Charlotte and Alexander had been betrayed.

They were herded into Nice's Excelsior Hotel with other prisoners and sent by train to the Drancy camp northeast of Paris on September 24, 1943. There were around fifty prisoners on that day's railway transport list from Nice to Drancy. Only two were from Villefranche: NAGLER, Alexander, and NAGLER, *née* Salomon, Charlotte.

Their train arrived at Drancy on September 27, 1943. The U-shaped camp building had been one of Paris's first high-rise apartment buildings. It was now surrounded by barbed wire and watchtowers. Charlotte was sent to the third floor, Alexander to the fifth. The windows had no glass and there was only straw on the concrete floors for sleeping. Water trickled into troughs for washing, and toilets were primitive. Food was scarce and terrible. Through the windows in the stairwell Charlotte and Alexander could see the streets of Drancy as they walked down the stairs to go to the courtyard. There was nothing to do there but talk and listen to rumors. They were being sent to labor camps in Germany. No, they were going to a special town for Jews. No, they would soon be in a place much nicer than Drancy.

On October 7, 1943, one thousand Drancy prisoners were awakened at four thirty in the morning. A half hour later they were put on buses, one group of fifty people per bus. Charlotte and Alexander were in group number seventeen. He was listed as a bookkeeper; she was listed as a graphic designer. They were given bread, sausage, and an egg and driven to the nearby train station. Each bus group of fifty people was kept together and loaded into a windowless, overcrowded train car intended for horses or cattle that was then locked from the outside. Their train was called Transport 60. The people on the train had no idea where they were going. In each car there was hardly any food, very little water, and one bucket to use as a toilet for all fifty people. They remained standing up; there was no room to sit or lie down. While the prisoners had nothing, another part of the train carried provisions intended for the German military: chocolate, coffee, sugar, potatoes, pasta, salt, beans, and canned vegetables, marked "not [to] be used for . . . prisoners."

Transport 60 arrived at a place called Auschwitz-Birkenau, in Poland, on October 10, 1943, before dawn. Once the passengers were on the platform, the men and women were separated and told to wait in line. They were disoriented from the inhumane conditions on the train, and exhausted and starving after the three-day-and-three-night trip. As each line moved forward the people were sorted into two groups. One group was kept alive to do slave labor. The second group was murdered without delay in the gas chambers, purpose-built rooms that were packed with people, sealed, and flooded with poisonous gas. When Alexander

Auschwitz extermination camp.

reached the head of the men's line, the man in charge pointed and motioned for Alexander to join a group of mostly men, young and reasonably healthy looking. When it was Charlotte's turn, she was directed to join a different group. She was with the elderly, the women with young children, and pregnant women like her.

Charlotte and her unborn child were sent to the gas chambers with all the others in her group.

Alexander, with prisoner number 157166 tattooed on his arm, died a few months later from the exhaustion of slave labor.

Theirs were three lives out of more than eighteen million people murdered by the Nazis during World War II. Six million were Jewish.

## CHAPTER ELEVEN

# SURVIVED

*We were amazed by the incredible progress
she had made.*

—Herr Professor Doktor Albert Salomon

In 1947, once private citizens could obtain French money, Dr. Albert Salomon and Paula Salomon-Lindberg traveled to Villefranche-sur-Mer and made their way to Ottilie Moore's villa. The Salomons had survived the war by remaining in hiding in the Netherlands. If only they had taken Charlotte with them.

Albert and Paula had come close to suffering the same fate as Charlotte and Alexander when they were arrested and sent to the Westerbork transit camp near Amsterdam in May 1943. Westerbork was the Dutch equivalent of Drancy, but some prisoners were kept there if they had special skills. Albert was put to work in the camp hospital and Paula volunteered to work there at night so that she could be near her husband.

The Nazis demanded that Albert sterilize Jewish women

prisoners, or be killed. Albert refused, but before the Nazis could carry out their threat, Paula reassured them that Albert would do exactly as they wished; all he needed were his own surgical instruments, clean clothes, and a day's leave to retrieve those items. Paula then used her vocal skills to impersonate a Nazi officer on the phone and to demand a longer period of leave from a higher official. As soon as they left Westerbork with their extended pass, they disappeared into hiding with the help of the Resistance. They changed location every night until they finally found a permanent place to hide in the countryside in the south of the Netherlands. Once the war ended, they settled in Amsterdam, having no wish to return to Germany.

After the liberation of the south of the Netherlands in spring 1945, Paula and Albert met an American scientist there and told him about Charlotte. He was able to travel to Nice, where he learned of Charlotte's death. They had thought Charlotte was safe in the South of France. Now they learned that their decision to send her there had cost their daughter her life.

Albert and Paula traveled to France, hoping that something belonging to Charlotte had been left behind. "It was the first time we returned to the place where we lost Lotte," Paula said. "All this time we thought she was safe there."

Ottilie Moore had returned to Villefranche from the United States, and she met the Salomons at her villa. They were surprised to see Charlotte's paintings hanging on the walls. She would not part with the paintings she had purchased from Charlotte, but Ottilie gave the Salomons *Life? or Theater?*, which Dr. Moridis had delivered to her after the war.

*Life? or Theater?* and one of Charlotte's self-portraits returned to Amsterdam with Paula and Albert. He had established a growing medical practice there, but Paula's concert career was over, although she did continue to teach singing. The war had robbed her of some of her best performing years. She had trained as a nurse in Berlin and was able to assist Albert in his practice.

They were astonished by Charlotte's art in the packages. "She was shy and timid," said Albert, "which is why I was so surprised when we saw her paintings later."

The Salomons' friend Otto Frank had shown his daughter Anne's diary to them and had asked them whether they thought it

Albert and Paula Salomon after the war.

was "of true value." In 1947, the same year that Paula and Albert went to the South of France on their search, Otto arranged to have portions of Anne's diary published as a book in Dutch called *Het Achterhuis* (*The Annex*). Sales were steady but interest increased with foreign-language translations. The Salomons had no idea what to do with Charlotte's *Life? or Theater?* They packed her masterpiece away for ten years.

But perhaps Anne and Otto Frank had planted a seed. *Charlotte: A Diary in Pictures*, with eighty art selections and a short biography of Charlotte by Emil Straus, was published as a book in 1963.

Straus had survived the war by hiding in the French Alps near Nice. He and Paula had been friends in Germany before the war, but the book nearly cost them their friendship. Paula wrote to their literary agent asking to change or remove sections Straus had written. "Stop the presses," Paula said in an urgent telegram. "Sections of text unacceptable." She listed her concerns in a long, detailed letter. Straus had described Paula negatively. He had painted too positive a picture of Ottilie Moore. He had left out Wolfsohn. Her list went on and on. "We are absolutely not in agreement with the present form." In the end, Straus's biography of Charlotte was edited to suit the Salomons' vision of how their daughter's life should be described.

Paula and Albert also helped choose the paintings for the book. They may have wanted to downplay Charlotte's focus on suicide. In her painting where Grandfather told her to just go ahead and kill herself, Grandfather's words were removed from the picture. The paintings selected for the book, along with the title, *Charlotte: A Diary in Pictures*, gave an Anne Frank diary–style presentation of Charlotte's life.

Everyone was missing Charlotte's point. By painting her life story she had also hoped to show that her suicide was not inevitable; that Wolfsohn's theories about survival and existence had worked for her; and that the happiness she found in creating art was "larger than all the suffering of humanity."

---

Alfred Wolfsohn also survived the war. He had escaped to London in 1939 with help from one of his students. After the war, he described Charlotte in a manuscript called *Die Brücke* (*The Bridge*). "It was hard to get through to her," he wrote. "She was unusually quiet and not inclined to open up and break through the wall she had built around herself."

Paula showed Wolfsohn the book *Charlotte: A Diary in Pictures* when she and Albert visited him in London. He was astounded when he saw the eighty paintings in the book, including several of him. He said that he had "misunderstood the impression that he had made on her." It remains unclear which other paintings from *Life? or Theater?* he may have seen or whether he knew that Charlotte had placed him in over four hundred scenes, painting more than two thousand appearances by him in her song-play. It is unlikely that Paula and Albert ever showed Wolfsohn Charlotte's thirty-five-page painted love letter to him.

## CHAPTER TWELVE

# INSPIRED

*We believe that her work is valuable for, and*
*important to, all mankind.*
—Paula Salomon-Lindberg

It is impossible to know when Charlotte and Alexander's wrapped parcels containing *Life? or Theater?* were first opened, but at some point, the pages became scrambled and were no longer in Charlotte's intended order. She had tried to prevent this by numbering the paintings or overlays and by putting a handwritten note inside one of the packages. "In order to facilitate the reader's understanding," she wrote, "an explanatory text has been added to several sheets. The numbering did not take place entirely according to the order—it is therefore advisable not to confuse the sheets and to look at the order in which they are now arranged." But her careful instructions were overlooked—or ignored.

Paula and Albert may have mixed up the pages when they opened *Life? or Theater?* in Amsterdam. The paintings were likely

Charlotte's instructions about the order of the paintings.

scrambled further in 1961 when Albert, Paula, and curator Ad Petersen at Amsterdam's Stedelijk Museum organized the first exhibition of Charlotte's art at their Fodor Museum annex. The exhibition included paintings from *Life? or Theater?* along with other art by Charlotte from Ottilie Moore's private collection. Some of Ottilie's paintings have since been lost and were perhaps destroyed when the villa was torn down and replaced by condominiums. Other paintings were donated to museums in Amsterdam and Israel by members of Ottilie's family and by some of the children that Ottilie rescued.

Charlotte's intended order for *Life? or Theater?* was probably confused even more in 1963 when Paula, Albert, and others worked on *Charlotte: A Diary in Pictures*, trying to make *Life? or Theater?* resemble Anne Frank's diary.

In the end, it took a museum curator, her assistant, and an

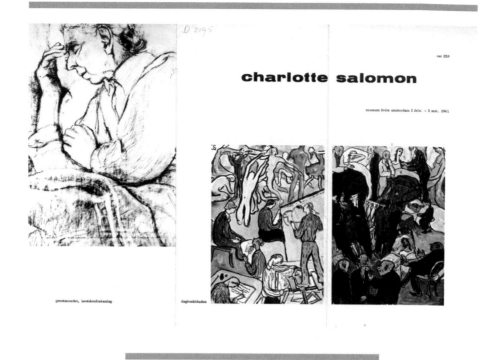

Brochure from the first exhibition of Charlotte's art, 1961.

entire house to rearrange the pages in a sequence close to what Charlotte may have intended. In 1971, Paula and Albert donated *Life? or Theater?* to the care of the Jewish Historical Museum in Amsterdam (known today as the Jewish Museum, Amsterdam). The museum's first task was to inspect and register every page. Curator Eva Ornstein-van Slooten and her assistant Judith Belinfante used at least five floors of a vacant house near the museum to lay out all the pages. Most of the transparent overlay sheets had become separated from the paintings they were meant to enhance and had to be rematched to their originals. Re-creating Charlotte's order for the art took six weeks. *Life? or Theater?* was as close as possible to her original concept.

Eva and Judith discovered that Charlotte had divided *Life?*

*or Theater?* into three sections that covered a twenty-seven-year period from 1913 to 1940.

**Part One** she called the "Prelude." Here she described her family's history and her own childhood, including Aunt Charlotte's suicide and the banning of Jews from public places. The paintings for this segment were often presented as rows of tiny scenes on a single page, almost like a comic book or graphic novel, as though Charlotte wanted to get as much information on a page as possible.

**Part Two** was the "Main Section" and was about Charlotte's adult life in Berlin. Here, her paintings were often close-ups of the characters, zooming in like a movie, and her color selections darkened. Wolfsohn appeared in nearly every scene.

**Part Three** was the "Epilogue" about her time in France and the horror and increasing danger of the war. Charlotte painted this section with loose swirls and flowing brushstrokes, and she brought back bright colors.

There were influences of silent films, ballad opera, art, and theater throughout her *Singspiel* (song-play). The German *Gesamtkunstwerk* (total work of art) may have been another influence for Charlotte. This art form blended elements like music, drama, poetry, dance, and visual art. Most *Gesamtkunstwerk* artists at the time were men, so Charlotte was an innovator, breaking new ground.

But there was still a troubling mystery about *Life? or Theater?* There were two big holes. In addition to the numbered paintings, the overlays, the rejected paintings, and the unnumbered paintings that Charlotte may or may not have included in her final version, there were sixteen pages of painted capital-letter text that didn't seem to fit anywhere. Researchers and scholars called

Charlotte painting in the garden at L'Hermitage.

them a postscript, but they lacked a clear beginning and page sixteen stopped in the middle of a sentence.

Two filmmakers discovered the answer to the mystery in the mid-1970s, but they were sworn to secrecy. By Paula.

When she and Albert had donated *Life? or Theater?* to the museum in 1971, they had held back nineteen painted pages, the pages that belonged before and after the museum's dangling sixteen. Paula showed the pages to Dutch filmmaker Frans Weisz in 1975, but only on condition that he promise not to reveal their contents. Weisz and his collaborator, Judith Herzberg, did not break their promise to Paula. It was only after Paula's death in 2000, at age 102, that the information Charlotte had painted onto those pages became available. She described her happiness while painting, her friendship with Ottilie Moore, her agony during Grandmother's decline, her misery living with Grandfather, and her decision to put poison in his omelet. The nineteen suppressed pages plus the museum's mysterious sixteen equaled Charlotte's painted letter to Alfred Wolfsohn.

"Above average."

Exhibitions of Charlotte's art continue to be organized worldwide, but it wasn't until 1981 that a complete edition of *Life? or Theater?* was published, almost forty years after Charlotte's death. It took another thirty-four years, until 2015, before a book was published that also included images of nearly all the overlays and Charlotte's painted letter to Wolfsohn. The letter he probably never saw was now available to the entire world.

Charlotte's story and her art have inspired novels, feature films, plays, documentaries, sculpture, a ballet, an opera, and extensive academic research and scholarship. Charlotte's life and creativity are examples of the strength, resilience, acts of resistance, and therapy that art, music, and writing can become during the darkest, saddest times. Her fortitude was astonishing in fending off her fear of suicide, the abuse from her grandparents, and the constant fear of arrest by the Nazis. She was able to transform her anguish into art. Her core belief, that the fear of *Selbstmord*—literally, "self-death"—could lead to self-revelation, played out in picture after picture.

Charlotte's genius, identified early on by Ottilie Moore, survives within every painting and every word of *Life? or Theater?* With it, Charlotte established herself as a true artist of the modernist period before time ran out. Not just *above average*, as Wolfsohn had suggested. Charlotte Salomon's *Life? or Theater?* is, as she said herself, "etwas ganz verrückt Besonderes."

"Something totally, wildly special."

# AUTHOR'S NOTE

## SHARING CHARLOTTE'S STORY

The first time I heard the name Charlotte Salomon was when one of my favorite artists, Maira Kalman, mentioned Charlotte in an interview. "The Charlotte Salomon paintings are very important to me," said Kalman, "and her work is really a profound influence."

I googled Charlotte and was hooked. I loved her painting style, her use of color, and her courage. I began researching her life and art. I discovered her painted memoir *Life? or Theater?*, a song-play with music, words, and art. I was moved by her determination to pursue her art in the face of racism, family suicides, abuse, and war. I also discovered that there were no books about her for young readers.

Charlotte's is a voice we cannot afford to lose; I wanted to tell her story for a new audience.

## CONCENTRATION CAMPS AND MY OWN FAMILY

I grew up in the southwestern United States—New Mexico—knowing a great deal about my mother's ancestors. They extend back to some of the earliest settlers in the state of Maine, and to England, Wales, Scotland, and Ireland before that. I knew very little about my father's side of the family.

During World War II, my father, Henry Wider, fought with the US Army in France and Germany, but he wouldn't talk about it. He also couldn't answer questions about his own family, apart from telling my sister and me that his parents had immigrated to the United States from Hungary. He said that the other relatives who stayed behind in that part of Hungary (present-day Ukraine and Romania) were "all killed in the war." They were Jewish, and like Charlotte, they were not safe.

My grandparents died many years ago, so I was not able to speak with them about the war, but when I was asked to expand my manuscript for this book, I decided to research my Jewish ancestry. I thought this might help me understand what Charlotte experienced, and I wanted to find out what had happened to my own mysterious ancestors. At the time of writing this book, my sister and I have learned that our great-grandmother, Sura Fuchs, was likely killed at Auschwitz—just like Charlotte—along with at least a dozen other aunts and uncles. We have also discovered survivors and their descendants and we continue to look for lost family.

After World War II there were no Jews left in the small town where my paternal grandfather was born and there are none there today. In 1944, the remaining Jewish residents were loaded into cattle cars and sent by train to Auschwitz.

They were all murdered there by the Nazis.

## BEING TRUE TO HISTORY

Charlotte Salomon has been the subject of books for adults about modern art, suicide, World War II history, and the Holocaust. Historian Mary Lowenthal Felstiner's remarkable 1995 biography, *To Paint Her Life: Charlotte Salomon in the Nazi Era*, remains a standard work for understanding Charlotte's life and times. The primary sources for my book were Charlotte's painted memoir

*Life? or Theater?* and her painted letter to Alfred Wolfsohn. I have chosen to trust her art and words. I supplemented this material with other Salomon scholarship and my own historical research. Little remains from Charlotte's personal life in terms of letters or photographs, but new details emerge from time to time. Wherever possible, I have incorporated this new information into my book. Sometimes in her art and writing Charlotte confuses time frames and makes historical and factual errors. Where I could, I substantiated Charlotte's approximations with historical facts. Memoir is only as accurate as our own memories.

# ACKNOWLEDGMENTS

Anton Kras, Senior Staff, Resource Center, Jewish Museum, Amsterdam, is one of the most patient people on the planet. He has answered a multitude of questions and guided me toward other experts. Also indispensable since I began my work on Charlotte Salomon in 2015 was Barb Messer, interlibrary loan librarian at Santa Fe Public Library, who tracked down books and documents that I would never have had access to otherwise.

Noted Salomon researchers and other scholars worldwide have been gracious and generous. Deepest thanks to Judith Belinfante, Charlotte Salomon Foundation; Toni Bentley, author; Darcy Buerkle, historian, Smith College; Mary Lowenthal Felstiner, historian; Kika Frouté-Moridis (Dr. Georges Moridis's daughter); Mila Ganeva, Miami University; Margret Greiner, author; Dana Plays, filmmaker, The University of Tampa (Ottilie Moore's grandniece); and Kerry Wallach, Gettysburg College.

Many historians, librarians, archivists, and translators helped extensively: Alix Agret, art historian, Musée Matisse; Ron Croonenbourg, translator; Caroline Deleu, Mathieu Thierry, and Marielle Victor, Archives départementales des Pyrénées-Atlantiques; Hervé Faure, Bibliothèque municipale de Nice; Dominique Giudicelli, Bibliothèque patrimoniale de Grasse; Jutta Haag, Landesarchiv Saarland; Linda Hutchings, Harold B. Lee Library at Brigham Young University; Antje Kalcher, archivist, Universität der Künste Berlin; Yves Kinossian, Archives départementales des Alpes-Maritimes; Claude Laharie, historian; Gracie Schild, translator; Anne Théry, Archives Matisse; Emile Vallés, Amicale du Camp de Gurs; and Bianca Welzing-Bräutigam, Landesarchiv Berlin.

Writing critique partners—and therefore friends of the highest order—Wendy BooydeGraaff, Eddie Edwards, Mary Helen Fierro Klare (1941–2019), Nikki Mann, and Amy Nielander contribute to my life and my writing in such enriching ways. Thank you.

Special thanks to two past critique partners, Alexandra Diaz and Mary Nethery, who insisted I query literary agents with my earliest version of Charlotte's story. How right they were.

Publishing industry professionals Jamie Bryant, Joanne Meiyi Chan, Elle Cosimano, Chris Eboch, Ellen Hopkins, Verla Kay, Elizabeth Law, Jenny McKay, Suzanne Morgan-Williams, Annie Nybo, Abigail Samoun, Michele Hathaway Tuton, and Sarah Zhang all guided and encouraged me along confounding publishing pathways.

Thank you to Kristin Allard, Sarah Johnson, Hana Nakamura, and the team at Norton Young Readers, who have contributed to Charlotte's story as much as the research did.

To family and friends Crystal Brown, Chantal Dubois-Perrier, Lisa Honeycutt, Shelly Lang, Julie Anne Peters, Lynne Ptacek, Kit Rosewater, Sharon Snyder, Natalie Spain, Sarah Wider, and Elaine Zimmer, life would not work very well without you.

And lastly, I want to thank the indispensable trio who saw potential. First, my agent Rosemary Stimola, founder of Stimola Literary Studio, who understood the magnitude of Charlotte's story for young readers long before I did. Next, Simon Boughton, head of Norton Young Readers, whose vision for this book continues to surprise me and to enhance the reader's experience. And my husband, Bill, whose support and encouragement are everything.

# CHARLOTTE'S FAMILY TREE

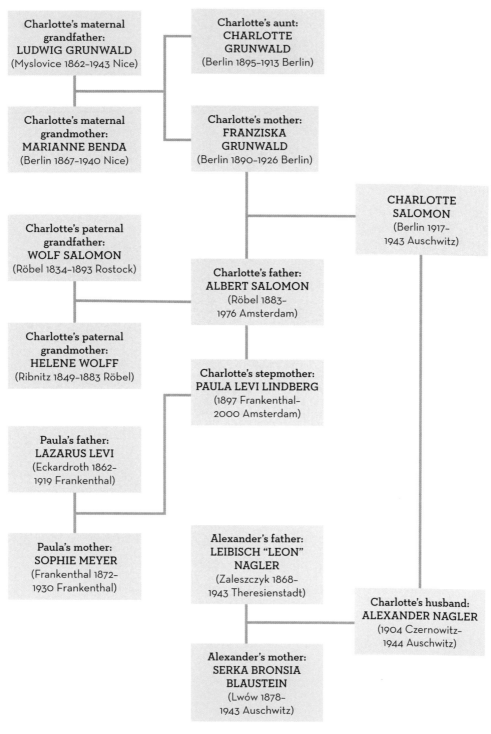

Charlotte's maternal grandfather:
**LUDWIG GRUNWALD**
(Myslovice 1862–1943 Nice)

Charlotte's aunt:
**CHARLOTTE GRUNWALD**
(Berlin 1895–1913 Berlin)

Charlotte's maternal grandmother:
**MARIANNE BENDA**
(Berlin 1867–1940 Nice)

Charlotte's mother:
**FRANZISKA GRUNWALD**
(Berlin 1890–1926 Berlin)

**CHARLOTTE SALOMON**
(Berlin 1917–1943 Auschwitz)

Charlotte's paternal grandfather:
**WOLF SALOMON**
(Röbel 1834–1893 Rostock)

Charlotte's father:
**ALBERT SALOMON**
(Röbel 1883–1976 Amsterdam)

Charlotte's paternal grandmother:
**HELENE WOLFF**
(Ribnitz 1849–1883 Röbel)

Charlotte's stepmother:
**PAULA LEVI LINDBERG**
(1897 Frankenthal–2000 Amsterdam)

Paula's father:
**LAZARUS LEVI**
(Eckardroth 1862–1919 Frankenthal)

Paula's mother:
**SOPHIE MEYER**
(Frankenthal 1872–1930 Frankenthal)

Alexander's father:
**LEIBISCH "LEON" NAGLER**
(Zaleszczyk 1868–1943 Theresienstadt)

Charlotte's husband:
**ALEXANDER NAGLER**
(1904 Czernowitz–1944 Auschwitz)

Alexander's mother:
**SERKA BRONSIA BLAUSTEIN**
(Lwów 1878–1943 Auschwitz)

# CHARLOTTE'S JOURNEY, DECEMBER 1938–OCTOBER 1943

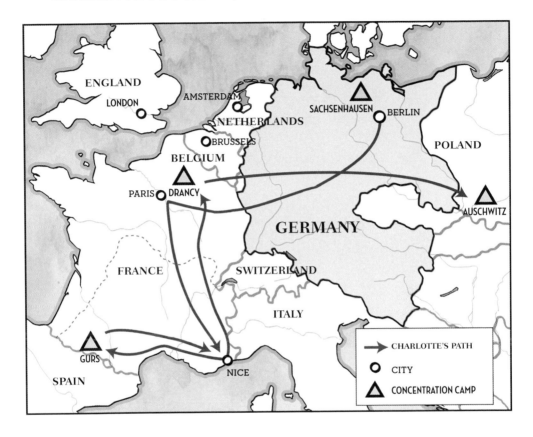

## TIMELINE

| | |
|---|---|
| **1917** | Charlotte is born in Berlin, Germany, on April 16. |
| **1918** | World War I ends in November. |
| **1921** | Adolf Hitler becomes the leader of the Nazi party. |
| **1926** | Charlotte's mother, Franziska, dies on February 22. |
| **1930** | Charlotte's father, Albert, marries Paula Lindberg in September. |
| **1932** | Franklin Roosevelt is elected president of the United States in November. |
| **1933** | Adolf Hitler is appointed chancellor of Germany on January 30. |
| **1938** | On *Reichskristallnacht*, November 9, Jews are attacked in Austria, Germany, and parts of Czechoslovakia. |

**1938**    Albert is arrested in November and sent to the Sachsenhausen concentration camp. Paula arranges his release.

**1938**    In December, Albert sends Charlotte to her maternal grandparents in Villefranche-sur-Mer, France, where she meets Ottilie Moore and, later, Alexander Nagler.

**1939**    Albert and Paula's passports are confiscated and they flee to Amsterdam in March.
- World War II begins on September 1 with the Nazi invasion of Poland.

**1940**    Charlotte's maternal grandmother dies in March.
- Nazi Germany continues to conquer much of Europe and invades France in May.
- Charlotte is required to report to the Gurs internment camp in the Pyrénées by June 1.
- Charlotte returns to Nice in July and begins work on *Life? or Theater?*
- German blitz begins against Britain in September.

**1941**    Ottilie Moore leaves France for the United States in September, taking ten children with her.

**1942**    Germany occupies nearly all of France by November.

**1943**    Grandfather dies in February.
- Charlotte marries Alexander Nagler in June and later gives *Life? or Theater?* to her friend Dr. Georges Moridis in Villefranche.
- Charlotte and Alexander are arrested in September and sent to Auschwitz—via Drancy—arriving on October 10.
- Charlotte and her unborn child are sent to the gas chamber on arrival at Auschwitz.

**1944**    Alexander dies of exhaustion at Auschwitz on January 1.

**1945**    World War II officially ends on September 2.

**1947**    Albert and Paula travel to France and discover *Life? or Theater?*

**1961**    The first of over seventy-five international installations of Charlotte's work takes place in Amsterdam.

**1963**    The first book about Charlotte is published.

**1981**    The first edition of *Life? or Theater?* is published that includes nearly all of the paintings.

**2015**    The first edition of *Life? or Theater?* is published including nearly all overlays and the painted letter to Alfred Wolfsohn.

# NOTES

## CHAPTER ONE: DENIED

3.........*"The artistic abilities of"*: Felstiner, *To Paint Her Life*, 39.

9.........**"Michelangelo is fabulous"**: Salomon, *Leben? oder Theater?*, M004329-b, Jewish Cultural Quarter (Amsterdam), https://data.jck.nl/search/?q=M004329.

10.......**"Only he who dares"**: Salomon, *Life? or Theatre?* (Waanders), 223.

10.......**"Oh I'm trying"**: Salomon, 225.

10.......**"If she's that keen"**: Salomon, 227.

13.......**"I really think you have"**: Salomon, 231.

14.......**"Ja, diesmal geht's"**: Salomon, *Leben? oder Theater?*, M004353, Jewish Cultural Quarter (Amsterdam), https://charlotte.jck.nl/detail/M004353.

14.......**"Yes, this time"**: Salomon, *Leben? oder Theater?*, M004353-b, Jewish Cultural Quarter (Amsterdam), https://data.jck.nl/search/?q=M004353.

14.......**"modest and reserved"**: Felstiner, *To Paint Her Life*, 39.

14.......**"present a danger"**: Felstiner, 39.

## CHAPTER TWO: GOVERNED

15.......*"No one can possibly"*: Salomon, *Life? or Theatre?* (Waanders), 82.

16.......**"I don't need any governesses"**: Salomon, 82.

16.......**"I know by myself"**: Salomon, 82.

16.......**"all kinds of naughtiness"**: Salomon, 82.

16.......**"do as I say"**: Salomon, 83.

## CHAPTER THREE: ABANDONED

27.......*"And I was left with"*: Salomon, *Life? or Theatre?* (Waanders), 184.

27.......**"something terrible"**: Salomon, 80.

32.......**"He is a lover of"**: Salomon, 93.

37.......**"Our home"**: Salomon, 98.

37.......**"Those new ones"**: Salomon, 98.

37.......**"but no one as much"**: Salomon, 98.

37.......**"Ist 'Sie' zu Haus?"**: Salomon, *Leben? oder Theater?*, M004236, Jewish Cultural Quarter (Amsterdam), https://charlotte.jck.nl/detail/M004236.

40 ......**"were both human"**: Salomon, *Life? or Theatre?* (Waanders), 192.

40 ......**"Aus—Raus—Aus—Raus"**: Salomon, 196.

42.......**"To Unite You Not"**: Felstiner, *To Paint Her Life*, 33.

43.......**"Just see your finals"**: Salomon, *Life? or Theatre?* (Waanders), 206.

43.......**"Spurred on by her"**: Salomon, 249.

## CHAPTER FOUR: COACHED

44 ......*"He's just as crazy"*: Salomon, *Life? or Theatre?* (Waanders), 397.

44 ......**"the prophet of song"**: Salomon, 258.

45.......**"greatest singer"**: Salomon, 266.

45.......**"going back to nature"**: Salomon, 273.

47........**"in order to be"**: Salomon, 287.

47........"my Madonna": Salomon, 323.

47........"She's my husband's daughter": Salomon, 325.

48........"noble specimen": Salomon, 402.

48........"profound subconscious fascination": Salomon, 479.

48........"Even if it drives me": Salomon, 479.

48 ......."has no particular artistic . . . something above average": Salomon, 481–82.

51........"elated . . . thoughts on her": Salomon, 482.

57........"turned out surprisingly": Salomon, 598.

57........"filled with grief": Salomon, 602.

57........"some day I'll find": Salomon, 605.

59........"virtually taken up": Salomon, 656.

59........"I've had enough of": Salomon, *Life? or Theatre?* (Waanders), 676. Author's own translation.

59........"I learned to concentrate": Felstiner, *To Paint Her Life*, 82.

## CHAPTER FIVE: EXILED

62........*"She was a sensitive"*: Salomon, *Charlotte: A Diary in Pictures*, II Charlotte.

64 ......."in order to": Salomon, *Life? or Theatre?* (Waanders), 705.

64 ......."L'Hermitage": Email from Dana Plays to the author, November 2, 2021.

65........"We headed to Amsterdam": Felstiner, *To Paint Her Life*, 99.

67........"renewed and clear": Felstiner, 101.

67........"in the world only": Salomon, *Life? or Theatre?* (Waanders), 723.

67........"like all the others": Salomon, 723.

67........"Bonjour, Lolotte": Felstiner, *To Paint Her Life*, 102.

68 ......."not of this world": Felstiner, 102.

68 ......."the Mute": Felstiner, 102.

68 ......."felt despair about life": Salomon, *Life? Or Theatre?* (Overlook Duckworth), 803.

69........"She was the only": Salomon, 803.

69........"Let's make a painting": Felstiner, *To Paint Her Life*, 131.

70........"Wherever she happened to be": Salomon, *Charlotte: A Diary in Pictures*, II Charlotte.

## CHAPTER SIX: STUNNED

72........*"Joy, O joy, divinest spark"*: Salomon, *Life? or Theatre?* (Waanders), 742.

72........"1889–1939: A little history": Salomon, *Leben? oder Theater?*, M002114, Jewish Cultural Quarter (Amsterdam), https://data.jck.nl/search/?q=M002114.

74........"Let art and nature": Felstiner, To Paint Her Life, 106.

75........"He just wanted to get": Salomon, *Life? Or Theatre?* (Overlook Duckworth), 803.

75........"I couldn't bear living alongside": Salomon, 803.

75........"have felt deeply disappointed": Salomon, 803.

76........"I knew nothing": Salomon, *Life? or Theatre?* (Waanders), 753.

77........"live for them all": Salomon, 764.

79........"an act of mercy": Salomon, 782.

79.......**"I can't stand it"**: Salomon, 781.

79.......**"My life began"**: Salomon, *Life? Or Theatre?* (Overlook Duckworth), 801.

## CHAPTER SEVEN: BROKEN

80 ......**"*I would not say*"**: United States Holocaust Memorial Museum, "Gurs: Personal Histories," Holocaust Encyclopedia, https://encyclopedia.ushmm.org/content/en/gallery/gurs-personal-histories?parent=en%2F4842.

81.......**"LES FEMMES RESSORTISSANTES"**: *L'éclaireur de Nice*, May 27, 1940, 3.

81.......**"Female German nationals"**: *L'éclaireur de Nice*, May 27, 1940, 3.

82.......**"in a railway car"**: Salomon, *Life? or Theatre?* (Waanders), 803.

82.......**"I'd rather have"**: Salomon, 803.

83.......**"Ça fait un bon"**: Vallés, *Itinéraires d'internés du camp de Gurs*, 62.

85.......**"To sleep again"**: Salomon, *Life? or Theatre?* (Waanders), 809.

87.......**"God[,] my God"**: Salomon, 812.

87.......**"I have a feeling"**: Salomon, 814.

87.......**"I saw the whole world"**: Salomon, *Life? Or Theatre?* (Overlook Duckworth), 801.

88 ......**"I believed strongly"**: Salomon, 801.

88 ......**"[I] was desperately unhappy"**: Salomon, 803.

89.......**"My love of drawing"**: Salomon, 801.

90 ......**"one must first go"**: Salomon, *Life? or Theatre?* (Waanders), 414.

90 ......**"I had to go deeper"**: Felstiner, *To Paint Her Life*, 130.

## CHAPTER EIGHT: OBSESSED

91 .......**"*She was very introverted*"**: Jewish Cultural Quarter, "Interview Paula and Albert Salomon for Pariser Journal, 1963," YouTube video, 6:16, posted March 25, 2015, https://www.youtube.com/watch?v=NlytljkojGo.

91.......**"We lived seemingly"**: Salomon, *Life? Or Theatre?* (Overlook Duckworth), 801.

91.......**"crushed by the proximity"**: Salomon, *Life? or Theatre?* (Waanders), 815.

91.......**"whether to commit suicide"**: Salomon, *Leben? oder Theater?*, M004922-a, Jewish Cultural Quarter (Amsterdam), https://data.jck.nl/search/?q=M004922.

91.......**"In the presence of"**: Salomon, *Life? or Theatre?* (Waanders), 818.

92.......**"loved him as much"**: Salomon, 821.

92.......**"in order to love life"**: Salomon, 821.

92.......**"to vanish for a while"**: Salomon, 822.

92.......**"I said that, if"**: Weisz, *Leven? of Theater?*

92.......**"The war raged on"**: Salomon, *Life? Or Theatre?* (Overlook Duckworth), 805.

93.......**"1913 One November"**: Salomon, *Life? or Theatre?* (Waanders), 47.

95.......**"Thus she would stand"**: Salomon, 178.

95.......**"Gott mein Gott"**: Salomon, *Life? or Theatre?* (Waanders), 812. Author's own translation.

99 ......**"Grandmother: Are you here"**: Salomon, *Life? or Theatre?* (Waanders), 723.

100.....**"three-color musical play"**: Salomon, *Life? or Theatre?* (Waanders), 43. Author's own translation.

100.....**"penniless scrounger"**: Pollock, *Charlotte Salomon*, 106.

100.....**"I was all the characters"**: Salomon, *Life? Or Theatre?* (Overlook Duckworth), 806.

100.....**"The creation of"**: Salomon, *Life? or Theatre?* (Waanders), 45.

101.....**"The police would not"**: Salomon, *Life? Or Theatre?* (Overlook Duckworth), 805.

101.....**"My happiness was at"**: Salomon, 805.

101.....**"eminent intellectuals"**: Felstiner, *To Paint Her Life*, 138.

103.....**"Charlotte was a sunny girl"**: Felstiner, 141.

104.....**"She painted all the time"**: Pécher, Four unpublished letters, D005046, Jewish Cultural Quarter (Amsterdam), https://data.jck.nl/search/?q=D005046.

105.....**"I left loneliness behind"**: Salomon, *Life? Or Theatre?* (Overlook Duckworth), 805.

## CHAPTER NINE: POISONED

106.....**"*The world needs people*"**: Salomon, *Life? or Theatre?* (Waanders), 574.

106.....**"I thought it was correct"**: Felstiner, *To Paint Her Life*, 155.

106.....**"leave right away"**: Felstiner, 155.

107.....**"Europe is to be combed"**: Felstiner, 140.

107.....**"I had to complete"**: Felstiner, 156.

109.....**"If he was Death"**: Salomon, *Life? or Theatre?* (Waanders), 821.

110.....**"The more that time"**: Salomon, *Life? Or Theatre?* (Overlook Duckworth), 805.

110.....**"Hitler's violent actions"**: Salomon, 805.

110.....**"Beloved friend"**: Salomon, 801.

110.....**"An incredible will"**: Salomon, 801.

110.....**"You said I was talented"**: Salomon, 801.

111.....**"Maybe by now"**: Salomon, 805.

111.....**"tore my grandmother"**: Salomon, 801.

## CHAPTER TEN: MURDERED

112.....**"*The more I saw*"**: Salomon, *Life? Or Theatre?* (Overlook Duckworth), 801.

112.....**"Mrs. Moore left me a friend"**: Salomon, *Charlotte: A Diary in Pictures*, IV The End.

112.....**"gentle and loyal"**: Felstiner, *To Paint Her Life*, 169.

112.....**"When Madame Moore"**: Felstiner, 169.

113.....**"We were somewhat close"**: Salomon, *Life? Or Theatre?* (Overlook Duckworth), 805.

113.....**"I had the desire"**: Salomon, 805.

114.....**"How gruesome our existence"**: Salomon, 801.

114.....**"In these chaotic"**: Salomon, *Charlotte: A Diary in Pictures*, IV The End.

116.....**"Keep this safe"**: Felstiner, *To Paint Her Life*, 236.

116.....**"the Jew Nagler"**: Salomon, *Selection of 450 Gouaches*, 21.

119.....**"not [to] be used"**: Felstiner, *To Paint Her Life*, 201.

## CHAPTER ELEVEN: SURVIVED

121.....*"We were amazed"*: Jewish Cultural Quarter, "Interview Paula and Albert Salomon for Pariser Journal, 1963," YouTube video, 6:16, posted March 25, 2015, https://www.youtube.com/watch?v=NlytljkojGo.

122.....**"It was the first time"**: Jewish Cultural Quarter, "Interview Paula and Albert Salomon."

123.....**"She was shy and timid"**: Jewish Cultural Quarter.

124.....**"of true value"**: Felstiner, *To Paint Her Life*, 224.

124.....**"Stop the presses"**: Buerkle, *Nothing Happened*, 37–39.

125.....**"larger than all"**: Salomon, *Life? Or Theatre?* (Overlook Duckworth), 805.

125.....**"It was hard to get"**: Wolfsohn, "Die Brücke," 1.

125.....**"misunderstood the impression"**: Braggins, "Legacy of Alfred Wolfsohn," 7.

## CHAPTER TWELVE: INSPIRED

126.....*"We believe that her work"*: Jewish Cultural Quarter, "Interview Paula and Albert Salomon for Pariser Journal, 1963," YouTube video, 6:16, posted March 25, 2015, https://www.youtube.com/watch?v=NlytljkojGo.

126.....**"In order to facilitate"**: Salomon, *Selection of 450 Gouaches*, 28.

## AUTHOR'S NOTE

133.....**"The Charlotte Salomon paintings are"**: Delson, "A Maira Moment."

# BIBLIOGRAPHY

## ARTICLES, INTERVIEWS, ORAL HISTORIES, AND ONLINE SOURCES

"Angel of Child Refugees Brings 10 of Them Here from Europe." *New York Post*, October 20, 1941. FultonHistory. http://fultonhistory.com/newspaper%2011 /New%20York%20Evening%20Post/New%20York%20NY%20Evening%20 Post%201941%20Grayscale/New%20York%20NY%20Evening%20Post%20 1941%20Grayscale%20-%204988.pdf.

"Anti-Jewish Decrees." British Library. Accessed May 17, 2017. http://www.bl.uk /learning/histcitizen/voices/info/decrees/decrees.html.

Appignanesi, Lisa. "Painting on the Precipice." *New York Review of Books*, February 22, 2018. http://www.nybooks.com/articles/2018/02/22/ charlotte-salomon-painting-precipice/.

Bentley, Toni. "The Obsessive Art and Great Confession of Charlotte Salomon." *New Yorker*, July 15, 2017. https://www.newyorker.com/culture/culture-desk /the-obsessive-art-and-great-confession-of-charlotte-salomon.

Braggins, Sheila. "Alfred Wolfsohn alias Amadeus Daberlohn: The Man and His Ideas" (lecture given September 16, 2007, at the Jewish Historical Museum, Amsterdam). Roy Hart Theatre Archives. Accessed July 17, 2018. http://www .roy-hart.com/amsterdam.lecture.htm.

———. "The Legacy of Alfred Wolfsohn." Roy Hart Theatre Archives. Accessed March 12, 2019. http://www.roy-hart.com/semsheila.htm.

Delson, Susan. "A Maira Moment: Kalman Retrospective Opens in NYC." Women's Voices for Change. March 11, 2011. http://womensvoicesforchange.org/tag /charlotte-salomon.

Erlich, Irène. "De Nice à Gurs." Camp de Gurs. Accessed August 24, 2021. http://www .campgurs.com/media/1472/ehrlicht-ir%C3%A8ne-de-nice-%C3%A0-gurs.pdf.

Felstiner, Mary Lowenthal. "Charlotte Salomon." Shalvi/Hyman Encyclopedia of Jewish Women. Jewish Women's Archive. Accessed February 24, 2015. https:// jwa.org/encyclopedia/article/salomon-charlotte.

Fischer-Defoy, Christine. "Paula Salomon-Lindberg und Charlotte Salomon—eine Liebesgeschichte in Bildern und Gesprächen." Berliner Wissenschaftlehrinnen stellen sich vor, Nr. 14. Zentraleinrichtung zur Förderung von Frauenstudien une Frauenforschung an der Frein Universität Berlin, 12 Mai 1992.

Jewish Cultural Quarter, Amsterdam: https://jck.nl/en/node/3396.

"Les femmes ressortissantes allemandes . . ." *L'éclaireur de Nice*. May 27, 1940.

Levitt, Aimee. "Charlotte Salomon's Life? Or Theater?: Painting For Her Life, Literally." Blogs. ChicagoReader. June 27, 2014. http://www.chicagoreader.com /Bleader/archives/2014/06/27/charlotte-salomons-life-or-theater-painting -for-her-life-literally.

Pécher, Marthe. Four unpublished letters to Gary Schwartz, 1981–1983. Jewish Cultural Quarter, Amsterdam. https://data.jck.nl/search/?q=D005046.

Pollock, Griselda. "An Event between History and the Everyday: The Secret of Charlotte Salomon's *Life? or Theatre?*" White Rose Research Online. https://

eprints.whiterose.ac.uk/81178/1/Pollock_An%20Event%20between%20
History%20and%20Memory%202014.docx.

———. "Recalling Charlotte Salomon." *Times Literary Supplement*, November 14,
2017. https://www.the-tls.co.uk/articles/charlotte-salomon-life-theatre/.

Rubinstein, Raphael. "Charlotte Salomon: A Visual Testament." *Art in America*,
January 1999.

Salomon, Albert. "Charlotte Salomon." Museum Fodor Amsterdam, 1961.

Schmetterling, Astrid. "Tracing the Life (or Theatre?) of Charlotte Salomon." *Issues
in Architecture, Art & Design* 5, no. 1 (1997).

Shendar, Yehudit. "New Exhibition: 'Life? Or Theater?'" *Yad Vashem* 42 (Summer
2006): 10–11. https://view.publitas.com/yad-vashem/yv_magazine42/page/10–
11.

Shendar, Yehudit, and Eliad Moreh-Rosenberg. "The Portrait and the Maiden:
New Charlotte Salomon Acquisition for the Art Collection." *Yad Vashem* 46
(Summer 2007): 10–11. https://view.publitas.com/yad-vashem/yv_magazine46/
page/10–11.

Sperling, Matthew. "The Turmoil and Talent of Charlotte Salomon." The Daily
Critic's Notebook. *Economist*, January 31, 2018. https://www.1843magazine
.com/culture/the-daily/the-turmoil-and-talent-of-charlotte-salomon.

United States Holocaust Memorial Museum. "Gurs." Holocaust Encyclopedia.
https://www.ushmm.org/wlc/en/article.php?ModuleId=10005298.

Wolfsohn, Alfred. "Die Brücke," In Christine Fischer-Defoy, *Charlotte Salomon—
Leben oder Theater? Das "Lebensbild" einer jüdischen Malerin aus Berlin
1917–1943*. Berlin: Das Arsenal, 1986.

Yad Vashem. "Non-Jewish Victims of Persecution in Germany." https://www
.yadvashem.org/holocaust/about/nazi-germany-1933–39/non-jewish-victims
.html.

## BOOKS

Buerkle, Darcy C. *Nothing Happened: Charlotte Salomon and an Archive of Suicide*.
Ann Arbor: University of Michigan Press, 2013.

Felstiner, Mary Lowenthal. *To Paint Her Life: Charlotte Salomon in the Nazi Era*.
New York: Harper Perennial, 1995.

Fischer-Defoy, Christine. *Charlotte Salomon—Leben oder Theater? Das "Lebensbild"
einer jüdischen Malerin aus Berlin 1917–1943*. Berlin: Das Arsenal, 1986.

———. *Paula Salomon-Lindberg—mein "C'est la vie" Leben*. Berlin: Das Arsenal, 1992.

Foenkinos, David. *Charlotte*. Paris: Gallimard, 2014.

Greiner, Margret. *Charlotte Salomon: "Es ist mein ganzes Leben."* Munich: Albrecht
Knaus Verlag, 2017.

Guillet, Jean-Luc. *Rafles Nice 1942–1944*. Nice: Baie des Anges, 2013.

Johnen, Stefanie. *Die Vereinigten Staatsschulen für freie und angewandte Kunst*.
Berlin: Metropol Verlag, 2018.

Laharie, Claude. *Le camp de Gurs: 1939–1945, un aspect méconnu de l'histoire du
Béarn*. Biarritz: J & D éditions, 1993.

Pollock, Griselda. *Charlotte Salomon and the Theater of Memory*. New Haven, CT: Yale University Press, 2017.

Salomon, Charlotte. *Charlotte: A Diary in Pictures*. New York: Harcourt, Brace & World, 1963.

———. *Life? or Theater? A Selection of 450 Gouaches*. Essays by Judith C. E. Belinfante and Evelyn Benesch. New York: Taschen America, 2017.

———. *Life? Or Theatre?* New York: Overlook Duckworth, Peter Mayer Publishers, 2017.

———. *Life? or Theatre?* Zwolle, The Netherlands: B. V. Waanders Uitgeverji, 1998.

Salomon, Charlotte, and Judith Herzberg. *Charlotte Salomon, Life or Theater?: An Autobiographical Play with Music*. Translated by Leila Vennewitz. Maarssen, The Netherlands: Gary Schwartz, 1981.

Schmetterling, Astrid. *Charlotte Salomon: Bilder Eines Lebens*, Berlin: Jüdischer Verlag im Suhrkamp Verlag, 2017.

Schramm, Hanna, and Barbara Vormeir. *Vivre à Gurs: Un camp de concentration français 1940–1941*. Paris: Librairie François Maspero, 1979.

Steinberg, Michael P., and Monica Bohm-Duchen, eds. *Reading Charlotte Salomon*. Ithaca, NY: Cornell University Press, 2006.

Vallés, Emile. *Itinéraires d'internés du camp de Gurs*. Pau, France: Editions Cairn, 2016.

## FILMS

Daval, Simon, and Jean-Francois Lami, dirs. *Pitchipoï*. YouTube video, 6:02, posted December 11, 2013. https://www.youtube.com/watch?v=ecIK1eYqJTc.

Jewish Cultural Quarter. "Interview Paula and Albert Salomon for Pariser Journal, 1963." YouTube video, 6:16. Posted March 25, 2015. https://www.youtube.com/watch?v=NlytljkojGo.

Weisz, Frans, dir. *Charlotte*. Concorde Film, 1981.

———. *Leven? of Theater?* Cine Mien, 2012.

# ADDITIONAL RESOURCES

## INTERNMENT AND CONCENTRATION CAMPS

*There are many online links to internment and concentration camp museums and memorials. Here are just a few:*

United States Holocaust Memorial Museum. "Auschwitz." Holocaust Encyclopedia. https://encyclopedia.ushmm.org/content/en/article/auschwitz.

———. "Gurs." Holocaust Encyclopedia. https://encyclopedia.ushmm.org/content/en/article/gurs.

———. "Sachsenhausen." Holocaust Encyclopedia. https://encyclopedia.ushmm.org/content/en/article/sachsenhausen.

———. "Westerbork." Holocaust Encyclopedia. https://encyclopedia.ushmm.org/content/en/article/westerbork.

Yad Vashem, The World Holocaust Remembrance Center. https://www.yadvashem.org/.

## CHARLOTTE SALOMON'S PAINTINGS

*To view more of Charlotte Salomon's art, see the website for the Jewish Cultural Quarter in Amsterdam, where every page of* Life? or Theater? *can be viewed, complete with all versos, overlays, unnumbered paintings, and Charlotte's musical references: https://jck.nl/en/node/3396.*

*Several of Charlotte's paintings that belonged to Ottilie Moore and members of her family can be viewed at the website of Yad Vashem, the World Holocaust Remembrance Center: https://www.yadvashem.org/museum/museum-complex/art/about/featured/charlotte-salomon.html.*

## RECORDINGS BY CONTRALTO PAULA SALOMON-LINDBERG

Sterkens, Jozef. "Paula Lindberg-Salomon, Alt 'Bist Du bei mir' Bach—piano Rudolf Schwarz, Berlin after 1933." YouTube video, 3:31, posted July 17, 2013. https://www.youtube.com/watch?v=sdX9mhbGljI

## SHORT INTERVIEWS OF ALBERT SALOMON, PAULA SALOMON-LINDBERG, AND OTTILIE MOORE

Joods Cultureel Kwartier. "Interview Paula and Albert Salomon for Pariser Journal, 1963." YouTube video, 6:15, posted March 25, 2015. https://www.youtube.com/watch?v=NlytljkojGo

## CHARLOTTE SALOMON GRUNDSCHULE

*School song about Charlotte Salomon, music and lyrics by students and faculty of the Charlotte Salomon Grundschule, Berlin. https://charlotte-salomon-grundschule.de/wp-content/uploads/2017/12/Charlotte-Salomon-Lied-2017.mp3.*

*Charlotte Salomon study group for fifth and sixth graders enrolled at the Charlotte Salomon Grundschule, Berlin. https://charlotte-salomon-grundschule.de/schulleben/angebote/charlotte-ag/*

# PICTURE CREDITS

# INDEX

*Note: Page numbers in italics indicate images.*